Contents

Political Philosophy

Alan Gewirth

THE UNIVERSITY OF CHICAGO

Sources in Philosophy

A MACMILLAN SERIES
Lewis White Beck, General Editor
THE MACMILLAN COMPANY
COLLIER–MACMILLAN LIMITED, LONDON

Library of Congress catalog card number: 65–11878

THE MACMILLAN COMPANY

COLLIER-MACMILLAN CANADA, LTD., TORONTO, ONTARIO

Printed in the United States of America

Sixth Printing, 1969

Introduction

I. WHAT IS POLITICAL PHILOSOPHY?

The central concern of political philosophy is the moral evaluation of political power. In its most important manifestation, political power is found in the state with its laws and government, which are formally and for the most part effectively supreme over all the other rules, institutions, and persons in any society. Political philosophy deals with the criteria for bringing these supreme political controls under moral control by subjecting them to moral requirements concerning their sources, their limits, and their ends or purposes.

It follows from this that political philosophy is a branch or application of moral philosophy. The relations between these two parts of philosophy, and between their respective subject-matters, have often been misconceived. It is sometimes said that moral philosophy deals with what is good or obligatory for the individual while political philosophy deals with what is good or obligatory for the state, or that morality is concerned only with the "inner" life of man while politics is concerned with his "external" acts. It is also sometimes held that morals and politics must be kept sharply separate. At least two arguments are adduced for such separation. One is that what is required for the national interest or for gaining political power is quite different from what is required for moral interpersonal relations. The other is that to view political conflicts in moral terms is to make them insoluble because this leads to moralizing in disregard of the relevant facts, and also because men are unwilling to compromise on what they conceive to be matters of moral principle.

These views, however, are largely mistaken. Moral philosophy does not deal only with the individual, since most if not all moral obligations are interpersonal in scope. Nor does moral philosophy concern itself only with "internal" motivations or intentions, since external acts also may be morally evaluated regardless of the specific motivations underlying them. And on the other side, political philosophy itself deals with motivation and character as well as with external acts. For example, in legal contexts questions of intention and knowledge are important in weighing criminal responsibility; and more generally, every political regime tries to obtain voluntary obedience and even conscientious commitment. Moreover, whatever be the aims of particular political agents or groups, their acts can and should be subjected to moral criticism simply because

1

they have such enormous consequences for human weal or woe. Such criticism does not necessarily entail dogmatic moralizing or an ignoring of the realities of power politics. On the contrary, there is definite moral value in settling political and other disputes by moral rules which stress mutuality of consideration as against the adamant stands of ideologues. The correct assessment of the applicability of such moral criteria demands, as a necessary prerequisite, a realistic awareness of relevant facts.

The right way to put the relation between moral philosophy and political philosophy seems to me the following. Moral philosophy deals with the most general considerations of moral values and obligations, while political philosophy deals with the application of these considerations to the moral questions of politics and the political order. Such application may vary in scope from very concrete to very abstract questions. Primarily, however, political philosophy is concerned to present, develop, and analyze general normative principles or criteria for answering moral questions of governmental or public policy. In carrying on this development and analysis, political philosophy sets forth a body of reasoned argument in justification of one or another position on these questions.

Because of this intellectual or rational concern, a political philosophy is not the same as an "ideology," where the latter word means the rationalizations which a group puts forth in support of its demands. Although most of the great works of political philosophy have reflected strong convictions on particular historical issues of major importance, and have often exerted great influence in shaping such issues, the significance of a political philosophy transcends its particular historical context. An ideology becomes a political philosophy only when it is concerned with general principles at the level of truth, validity, justification, and not merely at the level of propaganda, persuasion, or rhetorical victory. For these reasons, in making the selections in this book I have ignored ideological coverage of various "isms" which have agitated twentieth-century man, and I have likewise not tried to bring the selections "up to date." This is not to say that there is nothing new in recent developments. But if the student can think critically about the issues raised by Hobbes, Locke, and Hegel, for example, he should be able to handle the doctrines of a Hitler or a Stalin, a Gandhi or a Roosevelt, without much difficulty.

Although the central concern of political philosophy is to present and defend rationally grounded answers to normative moral questions about political power, it also has two other, subordinate aspects. One aspect is logical. As I have already suggested, political philosophy not only makes or presents general normative political judgments; it also engages in logical analysis of them. This involves an examination of the ways in which political judgments or evaluations can be supported or justified. It also involves an analysis of the meanings of concepts which figure importantly in political judgments, such as "state," "law," "government," "power," "authority," "justice," "right," "freedom," "equality." There is an intimate but complex relation between this logical task of political philosophy and its normative moral task.

The other aspect of political philosophy is factual or empirical. Political philosophy has to consult or at least take account of the facts dealt with by political science and related empirical social studies. The chief reason for this is epitomized in the famous Kantian doctrine that "ought" implies "can." If the political philosopher is to say what men's political relationships morally ought to be, then he must know what is possible in this area, for the possibilities limit the obligatorinesses. This is why political philosophers have always been concerned with basic factual questions about human nature and about the causal determinants of society and government. Whether or not politico-moral conclusions are directly derivable from the answers to such factual questions, the answers at least indicate the limiting conditions for such conclusions and they provide, together with appropriate moral premisses, the sufficient conditions for the conclusions.

The core of political philosophy, however, lies in its presentation and development of general normative moral criteria or principles for answering basic questions of political morality. Hence, we must now deal with two chief points: first, what are these basic questions; second, what are the general moral principles or criteria which political philosophy applies in answering them.

II. THE BASIC QUESTIONS OF POLITICAL PHILOSOPHY

Questions of political morality are questions about what men ought to do in relation to society and government, and about the right order and functioning of political power. Such questions may arise at many different levels, from the most concrete and particular to the most abstract and general. Logically, however, the answers to the more concrete questions are (with appropriate factual knowledge) deducible from the answers to the more general questions. Among general questions themselves, some are less general than others, and hence are logically answerable by reference to them. For example, questions about the limits of political obedience, about the rights of passive disobedience or of active revolt, are logically posterior to and answerable through positions taken on questions about the sources, limits, and purposes of political power. Consequently, the chief concern of political philosophy is with the most general moral questions of society and government, the questions whose answers are more or less directly decisive for all other questions of political morality.

What are these most general questions? We may list them schematically as falling on three major different levels, as follows:

1. *General question about society:* Why should men live in society at all?

2. *General question about government:* Why should men obey any government at all? Why should some men have political power over others?

3. *Specific questions about government:*

    a. *Source and locus of political power.* By what criteria is it to be determined who should have political power?

    b. *Limits of political power.* By what criteria is it to be determined what should be the extent of political power and what rights or freedoms should be exempt from political or legal control?

    c. *Ends of political power.* To the attainment of what affirmative ends should political power be directed, and what are the criteria for determining this?

These questions obviously fall into a hierarchy. Question 2 presupposes question 1, for there is no point in asking whether and why men should be under government unless they live together in society. And question 3 similarly presupposes question 2, for unless men are under government there is no point in asking what kind of government they should be under. As for the three specific questions about government, their formal exhaustiveness can be seen by noting that they deal, respectively, with the beginning, the middle or means, and the end of government (where these words refer not to temporal beginnings, and so forth, but to logical ones.) ¹ Another way to see both the exhaustiveness and the exclusiveness of the three specific questions is by noting that while all three questions deal with the rights of citizenship, the question of source or locus deals with the active rights, the question of limits deals with the negative passive rights, and the question of ends deals with the positive passive rights.

III. MORAL CRITERIA

We must now consider what are the general moral principles or criteria which political philosophy applies in answering these basic questions. Moral philosophers have distinguished two different kinds of general moral criteria. One kind is traditionally called *deontological* (from the Greek word *deon* meaning "duty" or "obligation"). On this criterion, one ought to do that which is inherently fair or just or right, as determined either by direct consideration of the act and its situation of itself, or by reference to some general formal principle (often one whose denial is self-contradictory). The other criterion is of the kind traditionally called *teleological* (from the Greek word *telos* meaning "end"). On this criterion, one ought to do that which will have the best consequences, do the most good, maximize utility (these three latter expressions being regarded as synonymous). Teleological criteria are often also called *utilitarian* ones, although historically only those teleological criteria are utilitarian which consider the consequences or utilities for society or mankind as a whole, as against, for example, *egoistic* criteria which consider the consequences only for the individual agent. We shall here confine ourselves for the most part to the utilitarian species of teleological criteria although, as we shall see, some philosophers, such as Hobbes, try to justify utilitarian criteria on an egoistic basis.

Both deontological and utilitarian criteria might justify the same course of action. Thus one might keep a promise, tell the truth, help the weak both because such acts are inherently right and because the consequences of these acts are better than the consequences of their alternatives. On the other hand, since the reasons or criteria which justify these acts are different, the acts justified by one criterion may well be opposed to the acts justified by the other. A teacher

¹ Note, similarly, the subtitle of John Locke's *Second Treatise of Government:* "An Essay concerning the True *Original, Extent,* and *End* of Civil Government."

may grade all his students impartially because this is inherently fair or just; but if he is concerned with maximizing happiness or utility he may well think he ought to give a higher grade to the student for whom this will mean more in the way of happiness. A person may pay his debts because doing so is inherently fair; but if he considers that he needs the money more than his creditor so that his not paying the debt will mean more overall happiness than his paying it, then on such utilitarian grounds he will think he ought not to pay the debt.

To avoid this conflict between the demands of justice (or fairness) and utility (or happiness), some philosophers have advocated a criterion called "rule-utilitarianism" as opposed to "act-utilitarianism." On the rule-utilitarian criterion it is not particular acts which are directly evaluated by reference to their consequences; rather, it is general rules involving whole systems or institutions which are thus evaluated. To revert to our previous examples, a rule-utilitarian trying to decide whether to grade his students impartially or to pay his debts would have to consider not the consequences of each of these acts by itself but rather the consequences of the whole institution or system of impartial grading or debt paying. It is the beneficial consequences of these institutions or systems as against the consequences of their alternatives that determine, for the rule-utilitarian, what acts should be done.

Even so, however, there remain potential conflicts between deontologism and rule-utilitarianism. For example, the rule that persons belonging to certain minority groups should be enslaved to work for the rest of the population, or should otherwise be discriminated against, is inherently unfair or unjust—that is, it violates the deontological criterion of distributive justice—but the rule might have more beneficial consequences, in the way of producing more goods for the total population, than its just alternative. And on the other hand, the rule that debts must be repaid or that the truth must be told, which would seem to satisfy the deontological criterion, might under certain circumstances have very harmful consequences for many innocent people.

One of the chief reasons why it is so difficult to relate deontological and utilitarian criteria in a cogent way is that the distinction between them is itself confused. At least five quite different distinctions are embodied in the deontological-utilitarian distinction as usually formulated. One is the distinction between *principle* and *consequences*, between regarding an act (or a rule) as inherently right, or right as a matter of principle, and regarding it as right because of its consequences.[2] The second is the distinction between *absolute* and *conditional* obligations, between regarding moral rules as binding unconditionally, with no exceptions permitted, and regarding them as binding only conditionally so that their requiredness can be overridden in certain circumstances. The third is the distinction between viewing moral criteria in terms of *obligations* or *duties* and viewing them in terms of *goods* or *values*. The fourth is the distinction between *formal* or *relational* and *material* or *substantive* criteria, between criteria that specify what is morally valid by reference only to a certain relation between persons (e.g., equality or impartiality) and criteria that specify a certain content (e.g., pleasure or happiness). The fifth is the distinction between *distributive* and *aggregative* criteria, between regarding an act (or a rule) as right because of the way it distributes something, and regarding it as right because it maximizes something.

Although these five distinctions are of course interrelated, no two of them are necessarily logically equivalent or even completely coextensive. The most important distinctions are the third, fourth, and fifth. Each of their poles may be viewed from the two standpoints of principle and of consequences, but this latter distinction is primarily one of emphasis; it does not mark a major differentiation so far as concerns morality. For while it is morally important to do things on principle, this cannot mean that morally relevant consequences, such as those vitally affecting welfare, should be ignored. And the distinction between absolute and conditional obligation, similarily, is not correlative with any of the other distinctions; when properly interpreted, it marks the difference between the supreme highest-order principle or principles and lower-order rules.

Let us, then, view "deontologism" and "utilitarianism" as constituted by one pole in each of the third, fourth, and fifth distinctions. "Deontologism" will hence refer to the *form* in which something is to be *distributed* as a matter of *duty*, while "utilitarianism" refers

---

[2] This distinction is itself often unclear, for it is by no means easy to differentiate what is solely "an act" from its consequences. When a man gets angry, picks up a gun, aims it, pulls the trigger, and kills a man, how many "acts" has he performed and with how many consequences? For a recent discussion of this question, see E. D'Arcy, *Human Acts* (Oxford: Clarendon Press, 1963), pp. 2–39.

to the *maximizing* of a *content* which is *good*. This is, indeed, a large part of the traditional meaning of the two criteria. From these definitions it emerges that when either deontologism or utilitarianism is emphasized to the exclusion of the other, we run into serious difficulties. For unqualified deontologism ignores what is to be produced: it could lead to an equal distribution of evils alone, according to some formula of impartial justice. And unqualified utilitarianism, while it emphasizes production of goods, ignores how they are to be distributed: it could lead to a drastically unequal distribution of goods, or a division between masters and slaves, so long as this resulted in maximal overall utility.

The right view on this whole subject, then, must combine utilitarianism and deontologism in some such way as the following. What ought to be produced is goods and avoidances of evils. How they ought to be distributed must take into account, first, all men's equal dignity; second, their equal opportunity to produce goods for themselves and others; and third, their unequal actual contribution toward such production.

Some aspects of this synthesis will emerge in the following sections when I present the ways in which political philosophers have applied utilitarian and deontological criteria in answering the basic questions of political morality. In making this presentation I shall be concerned, among other things, to classify positions rather than philosophers: a particular philosopher may be utilitarian on one point, deontological on another; and, as we shall see, each of these general criteria has various subvarieties. Before going on with this, however, we must briefly consider another moral principle which has traditionally been invoked in connection with political morality, that which goes by the name of "natural law."

An initial difficulty of dealing with natural-law theories is that they are quite diverse. Perhaps their chief emphasis has traditionally been that the "positive" institutions or "conventions" of human law and government are not morally self-validating, that they must be judged by, and must answer to, moral criteria which are therefore logically independent of and in this respect "antecedent to" the institutions. But in this sense, "natural law" adds nothing over and above what we have already seen in discussing deontology and utilitarianism as moral criteria for the evaluation of all human acts and institions, including political ones. The same point applies to the other contrasts often drawn between natural law and "positivism," such as that natural law is valid universally and not only for a special group, and that natural law presents moral principles which are validated by reason alone and do not depend for their validation on legal fiat. On these points, too, natural law adds nothing to what we have already seen in utilitarianism and deontology.

A further claim sometimes made in natural-law theories is that natural law is valid because it is based on the nature of things or on the nature of man, or both. This point, however, has already been considered above, in connection with the factual aspects of political philosophy.

In general, then, natural-law theories can be best understood as varieties of the criteria discussed above. Some natural-law theories are deontological, in that they set forth principles of distributive political justice which are held to be inherently obligatory. The principle of consent is an example of this. Other natural-law theories are utilitarian, in that they set forth principles which determine political obligations by teleological consequences, especially as these are related to human desires or social goals. St. Thomas Aquinas' "first precept" of natural law, that "good must be done and pursued, and evil avoided," is a prime instance of such a utilitarian principle. Such modern natural-law theories as those of Hobbes and Locke are, in their different ways, combinations of utilitarian and deontological emphases. In the eighteenth and nineteenth centuries, however, special circumstances caused utilitarianism to be conceived as being opposed to natural-law theories; I shall discuss this in the following section.

IV. WHY SHOULD MEN LIVE IN SOCIETY?

Let us now see how these moral criteria have been applied in answering the basic questions of political philosophy. We may first consider the general question about society: Why should men live in society at all? The most widely accepted answers to this question have been teleological ones, both egoistic and utilitarian. Men should live in society because of the obvious advantages derived therefrom. Without society men cannot survive, since society alone makes possible the division of labor and exchange of commodities which are necessary for the satisfaction of men's material needs. Many philosophers also stress that other kinds of goods besides biological and economic ones are made possible only by society, including those of human association itself: men value one another's company and friendship quite apart from any economic benefits they may derive therefrom. Other philosophers add that the cultivation of the moral and intellectual virtues is possible only through society.

Although the initial emphasis of each of these arguments is egoistic, referring to the good of each individual separately, they also become, by extension, utilitarian arguments referring to the greatest general good. That is, more total good is achieved if men live in society than if they do not. In this way, also, men come to have social "rights" and "duties" toward one another insofar as they can mutually help to fulfill one another's basic needs.

As we run through the list of utilitarian "goods" supplied by human society, we can also see the basis of an important distinction between two different types of utilitariansm. One type is *individualistic:* it views society as composed of elements, individual persons, who are basically complete even apart from society. They use society to fulfill their needs and desires, but these needs and desires can be specified independently of society, and society is at most a useful instrument for their satisfaction. Thus the goods stressed by the individualistic utilitarians are mainly such as are essentially localized in individuals or in small groups so far as their actual enjoyment is concerned, beginning with the goods of food, drink, clothing, security, and continuing on to aesthetic and intellectual goods.

Another type of utilitarianism is *organic,* or *corporatist:* it views the individual as constituted by, rather than as constituting, society in that the individual is basically incomplete, and indeed "unreal," apart from society. It is this point that Aristotle expresses in his famous assertions that "man is by nature a political animal" and that "the state is by nature prior to the individual." Hence organic philosophers hold that the very putting of the question, "Why should men live in society at all?" is unrealistic, for it seems to assume that men have an alternative, whereas in fact there is none. The goods stressed by organic philosophers are mainly the inherently social ones, that is, goods whose every enjoyment (and not just their production) directly involves a communal relationship—for example, the goods of friendship, of participation in social movements, and especially the social whole itself. Hence too the organic utilitarians stress far more the social duties of service to others by doing good to others, and far less the satisfying simply of one's own needs. It has often been pointed out that organic theories can degenerate into totalitarianism. Despite their stress on the social organism as a whole, organic thinkers often identify this with some special group such as a nation, an economic class, or a race. On the other hand, individualist theories can degenerate into callous egotism. Yet neither degeneration is inevitable, and each theory has an indispensable contribution to make to the philosophy of man and society.

What I have called organic utilitarianism is often conceived as quite opposed to utilitarianism. Historically, Hobbes, Hume, Bentham, Mill are classed as utilitarians in opposition to such organicists as Plato, Rousseau, Hegel, Marx. The reason for this can be seen if we look briefly at the history of modern political philosophy. The political and legal movement subsequently called "utilitarianism" arose in eighteenth- and nineteenth-century England among Bentham and his followers. These were philosophers of a markedly empiricist, individualist, and hedonist bent who were reacting against natural-law theories of the deontological type. Now the natural-law theorists, too, were mainly individualist and sometimes even hedonist; but the utilitarians' objection to them was that they were not sufficiently empirical: their invocation of "natural law" was often a capricious appeal to whatever they liked, since they supplied no empirical criteria for recognizing when something was or was not in accord with natural law. In eighteenth-century England, "natural law" had become a conservative rallying cry in defense of a host of institutions and practices which had long outlived their usefulness and which were barriers to social progress. By unqualifiedly identifying the good with pleasure or happiness, the utilitarians hoped to make obligations empirically calculable and to break the back of conservative resistance to change.

Now such organic philosophers as Rousseau and Marx were even more radical critics of the existing order than were the utilitarians; and Hegel too had a critical as well as a conservative side. But the nineteenth-century organicists reacted against the empiricist, hedonist, individualist aspects of the utilitarians' total doctrines, as well as against the "abstract," unhistorical character of both utilitarian and natural-law theories. These aspects, however, are not necessary components of utilitarianism in the generic sense defined above. The organicists are essentially utilitarian because they view what men ought to do by reference to the goods or values achieved thereby; but these goods, as we have seen, are now social rather than individualist—the locus of good is the economic class or the whole society rather than the atomic individual—and the goods are to some extent known by nonempirical means such as intuition or dialectical reason. It will be easier to see this utilitarian side of the organicists if we recall that a near-synonym of "utilitarian" is "teleological"; for in their different ways the organic philosophers emphasized the achievement of good ends as setting men's duties.

V. WHY SHOULD MEN OBEY ANY GOVERNMENT?

One type of historic answer to this second general question has been that there is no moral justification for government at all. Government is simply the instrument of rapacious power-seekers for the preservation and aggrandizement of their selfish interests. This view has always had supporters: sophists like Thrasymachus in ancient Greece, papalists like Gregory VII in the Middle Ages, Marxists and Machiavellian "elitists" in modern times, and anarchists in all ages. This answer, however, seems in many cases (although not in all) to confuse the question of what motivates seekers after political power with the question of what justifies the institution of political power.

The words "Why should" in the general question about government are susceptible of either a utilitarian or a deontological interpretation. On the former interpretation they mean: "What ends or goods justify that some men have political power over others?" On the latter interpretation they mean: "What makes it fair or just that some men have political power over others?"

Let us first consider the utilitarian interpretation of the question. The answers have been of two different types, one leaning more toward organicism, the other more toward individualism. The organicist type of answer assumes as its context a whole society, and it answers the question of the justification of political power by reference to the needs of that society. Men living in association with one another must have uniform rules to live by, and there must be more or less explicit agencies for making, interpreting, and enforcing the rules. Some organicists emphasize tradition and history as more important sources in this connection than explicit rule-making agencies. In any case, there is agreement that without government there will be disorder and unpredictability, conflicts of interest will be unresolved and strife will result, thereby removing the goods or advantages of society. A graphic depiction of this point is presented in Hobbes's portrayal of the "state of nature" (by which is meant not a certain historical or prehistoric epoch but rather a hypothetical one: what men's condition would be like in the absence of positive law and government). Although most organicists do not accept the "state of nature" method of depicting the need for government (Plato and Rousseau are exceptions), Hobbes's answer that this condition would be a "war of all against all" is only a more vivid and vehement statement of a point which, to one degree or another, is accepted by most political philosophers.

There still remains, however, the question of the relation between the needs of society and the acquiescence of the individual. Since government involves the potential coercion of the individual, are the goods of society as a whole a sufficient justification for the individual's acceptance of such coercion? This consideration leads to another, more individualist type of utilitarian answer to the general question about government. This answer assumes as its context not the needs of society but the desires of the individual; that is, it tries to show that what is for the public interest is also for the individual's private interest. The context here usually includes an assumption of psychological egoism; as Hobbes puts it, "of the voluntary acts of every man, the object is some good to himself." The problem then becomes: what good does it do a man to accept the restraints of government and the rules of justice? The answer is given, as before, through the concept of the "state of nature," but now focusing on the individual's desires rather than on society's needs: without government and justice there would be constant strife, attacks on person and possessions would be very difficult to control, and the individual's life would be "solitary, poor, nasty, brutish, and short." The justification of government to the individual, therefore, is private or self-interest, in that government is the necessary condition of the individual's self-preservation and security.

It seems clear, however, that this individualist-utilitarian (or egoistic) answer does not establish its point. For, if we take Hobbes's (or Hume's) egoistic man, while it is certainly not to his interest that he be in a "state of nature" situation where there is no government or law, is it not more to his self-interest that *everyone else* obey the law while he does not? If self-interest is the only moral basis of one's duty to be just, then doesn't one have a moral right to be unjust whenever this is to one's self-interest and one can get away with it? This was the problem which Plato put into the mouths of Glaucon and Adeimantus in the second book of the *Republic,* and he provided an answer different in a crucial respect from that of Hobbes and Hume. The answer was that the change from an apolitical situation without justice to a situation where the rules of justice are made fully operative must be accompanied by a corresponding psychological change in the individual himself. He will no longer have the same egoistic impulses with which he began, desiring the satisfaction of those impulses regardless of their impact on other men; instead, he will recognize that his true interest consists in voluntarily conforming to the requirements of justice in the sense of an impartial order which apportions rights and duties according to merit. Such conformity is to the individual's true interest because otherwise his soul is sick. Plato is thus explicitly the ancestor of the doctrine that moral virtue consists in mental health (*Republic* iv. 444). This answer was echoed by Rousseau; and it marks the doctrine of the organic utilitarians as against the individualistic ones, for it depends on viewing the good of the individual as inherently constituted by the good of society.

It will be noted that there is a sense in which for Plato and Rousseau, as for Hobbes and Hume, the justification of government is self-interest. The difference comes in the view of the "self" and its "interest." Hobbes and Hume try to maintain the original self basically unchanged, with its drive for power and possessions. Plato and Rousseau, on the other hand, recognize that the justification of government requires a different kind of self, one whose ruling influence is not the drive for aggrandizement of its impulses without regard for objective deserts or the rights of others. This difference in the conception of the self is sometimes put as a distinction between an "empirical" self and a "transcendental" self. The distinction may also be put, however, as a contrast between an "egocentric" self and a "reasonable" self.

Philosophers of the reasonable self include not only organicists like Plato, Rousseau, and Hegel but also those whom I shall call *natural-rights deontologists,* like Locke and Kant. (Locke also has a utilitarian side, which I shall ignore for the present.) These deontologists do not, like the organicists, locate the good in society as a whole; rather, they emphasize inherent rights of the individual which for the most part cannot justly be infringed by government, and whose equal protection is the purpose of government. (I shall discuss the basis of this egalitarianism in the next section). But like the organicists, and unlike the individualist utilitarians, the natural-rights deontologists emphasize that the self is not intrinsically dedicated to its own gratification regardless of the rights of other men or the needs of society.

There are, then, at least these three different positions on the justification of the individual's duty of obedience to government. The individualist utilitarians, insofar as their basis is purely egoistic, justify too little, because on the basis of egoism the individual's duty to obey government cannot sufficiently be established. The organicist utilitarians, on the other hand, justify too much, because they tend to swallow the individual's desires into the social whole, in that they view the rational will as aiming not at its own interest but only at the interest of society; hence they leave the individual no rights against the whole. The natural rights deontologists fall between these extremes, because they view the reasonable self as aiming at its own interest but also as recognizing the equal right of others to an equal consideration of their interests, so that the individual's duty to obey government is neither contingent solely on satisfaction of his own private interests nor necessitated in disregard of his private "reasonable" interests. This question, then, turns in large part on the relation between the individual's private interest and the public interest. For the organic utilitarians the private interest is defined in terms of the public interest or the common good conceived as something over and above private interests. For both the individualist utilitarians and the natural rights deontologists, on the other hand, public interest is defined in terms of private interests. The deontologists, however, insist that these private interests must be reasonable in the sense indicated above, so that the public interest is the formal pattern of equal consideration among the private interests. But the individualist utilitarians define the public interest as the sum of private interests with no such restrictions on the reasonableness of the "interests"; hence they are faced with the problem of conflicts among private interests, which they solve in purely aggregative terms of what policy will do the most overall good or the least overall harm. The distributive question of what rights the individual may have as against the maximizing of social goods or utilities is thus left without a distinct answer by the individualist utilitarians as well as by the organicists.

All three of these groups hold that government must "do justice." For the natural-rights deontologists, however, justice is mainly formal: it is the impartial order or framework of rules, preferably minimal and largely negative, which give each person an equal freedom to pursue his own interests so long as he does not infringe the conditions of that pursuit in others. The chief justification of government is that it assures this impartial order, especially by giving authoritative interpretations and enforcement of the general rules of justice in particular cases. For the organicists, on the other hand, the rules of justice are affirmative, maximal, and substantive rather than formal: justice consists in each person's fitting into the social context in the way in which he can make the best contribution to the good of the whole. The main function of government is to coordinate and otherwise assist these contributions. For the individualist utilitarians, somewhat like the organicists, justice is a means to overall utility, but somewhat like the natural-rights deontologists, they tend to conceive justice more in negative than in positive terms, as what is needed to prevent social harm rather than to do good; hence they usually view the function of government as coercive and repressive.

There is a corresponding variation as to the nature of the "reason" which grasps the principles of justice. For the natural-rights deontologists this reason is equally in each individual; and just as justice is formal, so reason too is formal, using the principle of noncontradiction to establish necessary relations between the equal rights of individuals. Kant's categorical imperative is the most famous example of this; but a passage which Locke quotes from Hooker (*Second Treatise*, section 5) exhibits a markedly similar formalism. For the organicists, on the other hand, reason is substantive rather than formal, and is not found equally in each individual; its locus is more collective than distributive, for it characterizes the immanent structure of social institutions and is the possession of a whole class or society whose members exhibit it unequally. The self is "rational" in that by fitting into the social context, it can grasp and conform to the social purpose or public good to the extent appropriate to its station. For the individualist utilitarians, reason is calculative of means to ends, and hence has no inherently moral significance except insofar as the calculations of self-interest may coincide with what is for the public interest.

Thus far we have been considering the varying answers given to the utilitarian interpretation of the general question of the justification of government. But it will be recalled that there is also a distinct, deontological interpretation of this question. The point of this interpretation is that government as such has an essentially *distributive* aspect, in that it not only produces results for a whole society but it also entails a distribution of power between rulers and ruled: some men have political power over others. For the deontologists, then, the question still remains: what, other than its good consequences, can make this distribution just? Are some men entitled to govern others simply because such government is for those others', or even for the common, good?

Now this general question is closely related to, but not identical with, the specific question of who should have political power. The question of what can justify the distribution of power between rulers and ruled in general is not the same as the specific question of how that power should be distributed. Nevertheless, I shall now take up this distributive aspect of the general question together with the specific question of the allocation or distribution of power, since the deontologists (although not the utilitarians) give largely the same answer to both questions.

VI. WHO SHOULD HAVE POLITICAL POWER?

There have been three chief kinds of deontological answer to this specific question and the related general one. In modern times the most prominent answer has been that of the natural-rights deontologists. This is the principle of consent: no one ought to have political power over another unless the latter has consented to it. There is an important difference, however, between the answers to the general and the specific questions with respect to the subject of consent, i.e., who it is that must give consent. To the general question of the justification of political power as such, the answer is that consent must be given by each individual subject to it. The central argument is that political obligation is a species of moral obligation, and no individual can have any moral obligation unless he has imposed it on himself. In this respect consent is assimilated to the idea of a promise: to consent to someone's having political power is to give him a promise of obedience; without this promise there is no obligation to obey. A further crucial component in the consent principle is the idea that all men are by nature free and equal, so that the only thing that can justify the political power of one man over another is that the latter has consented to it.

What, however, does it mean to say that all men are naturally free and equal, and how is this proved? In modern political philosophies this doctrine is usually presented in connection with the concept of the "state of nature" which we have already met with in the preceding section. But in this context the doctrine of men's natural freedom and equality is to some extent simply a tautology. For if we define the state of nature as the condition of man in the absence of positive law and government, then it follows by definition that in such a condition men would be politically "free" in that they would be subject to no government or laws, and they would be politically "equal" in that no one would have political power over anyone else. Most philosophic proponents of natural freedom and equality, however, intend something more than this, but what they intend varies. Hobbes means by it that all men are equally capable of inflicting physical harm on one another, and that all men have a kind of rough and ready "prudence" which makes them equally capable of learning from experience in matters to which they apply themselves. Locke's, however, is the more usual interpretation. According to this, the doctrine of men's natural equality is not primarily factual but rather moral: all men are equally endowed with certain basic rights to life, liberty, and the fruit of their labors. The basis of this equality of rights, in turn, may be of different kinds. One basis is theological, deriving from the ancient Stoics and incorporated into Christian doctrine. According to this, the universe is a divine order in which all rights and duties derive from God, and all men are equal because they occupy the same "rank" in this universe. Another, more strictly philosophic, basis involves an appeal to man's moral rationality: all men (with but few exceptions in the cases of lunatics and idiots) are capable of knowing the moral law and governing their actions by it. Hence they are able to recognize the principle of justice, that the rules they wish others to observe in relation to them, they must also apply to others. This is emphasized in Hooker, Locke, and Kant.

It will have been noted that this deontological justification of political power by consent is along quite different lines from the utilitarian justification in terms of government's maintaining order and securing other goods. The justification by consent refers not to the valuable ends or consequences of government but rather to means or origins, to the inherent justice of the distribution of power. In actual practice, however, these diverse justifications by consent and by utility have often been fused. For most political philosophers of consent have also held that consent is given for a purpose: that there may be political society which provides security and justice. We can see the logic of this combination if we recall our discussion in Section III of the necessity for having both formal-distributive (deontological) moral criteria and substantive (utilitarian) ones. There is no point in providing for just distribution of power between rulers and ruled unless there is some good purpose to be achieved by the power.

The metaphor of consent most usually employed in this purposive connection is that of a "social contract" or "compact" or "covenant" or "agreement." It is this which effects the transition from the apolitical "state of nature" to civil or political society. In Hobbes and Locke the social contract is entered into by all the individuals to form a political society, but the specific allocation of political power to a ruler or government is not itself accomplished by the contract: for Hobbes this allocation is accomplished by a "gift," while for Locke it is rather a "trust." In Rousseau, on the other hand, the contract accomplishes both the establishment of political society and the allocation of sovereign power to the "general will," the whole community thus formed (although the question of "government" is subordinate, for government only applies laws which it does not make; and government, as against sovereignty, is not established by a contract). In other writers, the contract is at least in part a specifically "governmental" one in which the people agree to obey a ruler in return for his agreeing to rule justly. In all these cases, however, the consent or contract envisages the attainment of certain purposes or goods, and hence it is in this respect utilitarian.

Contract theories have been severely criticized by both individualist and organicist utilitarians, such as Hume and Hegel. Both groups decry the unhistorical, fictional character of the contract. This, however, is in part a misunderstanding: like the "state of nature," the "social contract" is intended not as a historical event but as a logical construct for emphasizing the voluntary, consensual, purposive character of political society. It is this very point, however, which the critics also condemn; they point out that men are born into political society and cannot "contract out" of it. How, then, can the consent-deontologists' assumption of original or basic freedom be reconciled with the restraints actually and necessarily imposed by political society?

It will be best to consider this problem in the context of the consent-deontologists' answer to the specific question of who should have political power. The answer is still consent; however, it is no longer the consent of each individual but rather the consent of the majority which determines the specific allocation and conditions of political power. Now this transition from individual consent to majority consent raises serious problems. For it means that at the specific level of the actual operation of government, men no longer impose obligations on themselves, they no longer obey only themselves, since they have to go along with the majority on who should rule, whether they want to or not. Hence we find various fictional devices employed to make it appear that the original freedom and autonomy are still preserved. Thus Hobbes (who in this respect is a deontologist) declares that "criminals have consented to the law by which they are condemned." Locke constantly writes as if the individual's "own consent" were entirely the same as "the consent of the majority" (see, for example, Section 140). And Rousseau insists that sovereignty cannot belong to any majority or to anything less than the whole people, because each individual is equally a part of the people, and only if the sovereignty remains in the people does each individual "still obey himself alone and remain as free as before." In other words, popular sovereignty entails individual freedom and consent in the sense of autonomy or self-determination.

On the specific question of the allocation of political power, as well as on the general question of why there should be this power, the deontological answer in terms of consent is fused with a utilitarian answer. The consent of the majority is justified as the source which allocates political power not only because this is just but also because of its having better consequences than any alternative. To remain with individual consent would mean anarchy, since no government would be possible if each individual had to consent before a specific allocation of political power was authorized. Moreover, the consent of the majority is more secure than having some exclusive minority control the allocation of power, for the minority might turn this power to its own private interests in disregard of the common interest.

Nevertheless, this utilitarian answer is distinct in principle from the deontological one. For if majority consent were justified only by its having the best consequences, then if those consequences could be achieved without majority consent, the latter would have no other justification. The deontological answer, on the other hand, does not make the institution of majority rule thus contingent on consequences.

Although the consent principle has been emphasized by many modern political philosophers, it was not unknown in ancient and medieval times. In the Middle Ages, however, a different kind of deontological justification of government in general was widely current. This is that "the powers that be are ordained of God" (Rom. 13:1). Here again a utilitarian basis was attached: the reason why God ordained that there be governments is that these were needed as punishments and remedies of original sin.

As for the specific allocation of power, these theological deontologists eventually came to hold that, since the pope is God's vicar, the actual holder of political power must be approved, if not actually designated, by the pope.

In the ancient world, especially among the Greeks, there was still another deontological justification both of government in general and of the specific allocation of political power. This held that there is a "natural" difference of status between men, in that some men are by nature intellectually superior to others, and hence have an inherent right to rule them. Plato's doctrine of philosopher-kings in the *Republic* and Aristotle's doctrine of natural rulers and natural slaves in the *Politics* are the two most famous examples of this. Aristotle also indicated that absolute kingly or aristocratic rule for life would be justified if there is "some one person, or more than one . . . whose virtue is so preeminent that the virtues or the political capacity of all the rest admit of no comparison with theirs." As in the other two cases of deontological principles just noted, here too utilitarian arguments accompany the deontological ones. But the "goods" to which these utilitarian arguments appeal as justifying the allocation of political power to an elite are far less diffuse and egalitarian than the medieval and modern ones; they involve rather more restrictive, differentiated, aristocratic ends of the Idea of the Good (Plato) or "virtue" (Aristotle), consisting in the maximal development of moral and intellectual excellences.

What is the relation between the egalitarian doctrines of the modern consent-deontologists and the hierarchic, anti-egalitarian doctrines of the ancient Greeks? This question involves many subtle problems. Locke, for example, recognized too that men are unequal in most empirically ascertainable ways (see *Second Treatise,* sec. 54), yet he certainly did not think that this gave the superior men the right to rule the rest. Aristotle himself, despite his emphasis on inequality, stressed at one point that the many when assembled together are better judges on questions of policy than the few, among other reasons because the recipients or users of something are better judges of its adequacy than is the maker of it. Hence general good judgment is a better criterion for allocating political power than is expertise. The difference between the egalitarian and the hierarchic positions derives in part from whether one thinks of the state as an instrument for the maximal development of the moral and intellectual virtues or as having a less aristocratic function; for the criteria of politically relevant equality will vary with this. But in addition, there is a different assessment of individual personality and capacities. When Aristotle said that "the slave has no deliberative faculty at all" (*Politics* I. 13. 1260a 12), he might have been right if he was describing the results of the brutalization of men brought about by the institution of slavery. But Aristotle distinguished such "conventional" slavery from the "natural" slavery which he held to involve an inherent incapacity to deliberate. In intending his statement in this way, however, he was making a factual, empirical mistake similar in principle to that involved in his erroneous assertion that women have fewer teeth than men (*History of Animals* II. 3. 501b 20).

This divergence between the modern consent-deontologists and the ancient status-deontologists also involves a difference concerning the nature of the state, parallel to the difference we noted in Section IV between the individualistic and organicist utilitarians. Where for the consent theorists the model of the state is an "artificial" contract between free and equal individuals whose purposes the state exists to serve, for the status theorists the model of the state is a "natural" organism in which the "higher" parts must rule the lower for the good of the whole.

Let us now turn to the utilitarians' answer to the specific question of who should have political power. All utilitarians answer this question by reference to the attainment and maximizing of goods; but there is an important initial difference between what may be called "merit-utilitarianism" and "result-utilitarianism." According to merit-utilitarianism, the criterion which should determine the distribution of political power (as well as of other goods) is merit in contribution to the production or maximizing of goods, that is, the common good. Thus Aristotle holds that those who contribute most to the end or purpose for which the state exists should have supreme power in the state. On this view it can be seen that the deontological criterion of distributive justice is subsumed under the utilitarian criterion of maximizing goods. According to result-utilitarianism, on the other hand, the distribution of political power should be determined solely by the criterion of what will best serve to maximize goods, with no regard to relative merit in contributing to such maximization.

Related to this contrast but not identical with it, there is a further difference. In applying his merit-utilitarian criterion of distributive justice to the question of who should have political power, Aristotle emphasizes that different kinds of states have different basic values or ends, so that the specific criteria for allocating power must vary accordingly. The basic value of democracy is freedom; of oligarchy, wealth; of aristocracy, virtue. Hence a democracy gives supreme power to the many who are poor but free, an oligarchy gives it to the wealthy; an aristocracy, to the virtuous. This emphasis on qualitative differences, which J. S. Mill was later to reiterate, may be called "qualitative" or "specific" utilitariansm, as against the purely "quantitative" or "general" utilitarianism which emphasizes solely the maximization of goods with no qualitative specification of differences among the goods or the ends for which they are to be maximized. Hence, although Aristotle holds that virtue is the best criterion for allocating political power, he recognizes the justice of alternative criteria in different kinds of societies according to their basic values and other circumstances.

Most utilitarians, both individualist and organic, are result-utilitarians, but some emphasize specific, others general good results, and their views about who should have political power vary accordingly. Thus for Hobbes the supreme good is self-preservation, the supreme evil death and civil war; hence he advocates an extremely powerful sovereign to maintain order, and leans heavily toward absolute monarchy. This is in contrast with Locke, who has a utilitarian as well as a deontological side; for him, tyranny is a worse evil than civil war. Consequently, the supreme power always remains in the people, although it is to be exercised only when the government, or legislature, violates its "trust" of preserving individual rights and acting for the public good. Later individualist utilitarians, like Bentham and James Mill, emphasize general maximal utility for the whole society without any reference to distinct individual rights. Hence they advocate democratic government, but this involves their arguing (with doubtful logic) from the psychological-egoistic premiss that each person aims at his own greatest happiness to the conclusion that in a democracy, where everyone shares in governmental power, the government will necessarily aim at the greatest happiness of the whole community, or of the greatest number. J. S. Mill, as a qualitative utilitarian, upholds representative government on the ground that it fosters moral and intellectual development in the members of the society. But the same qualitative criterion leads him to advocate many restrictions on universal egalitarian suffrage.

For the organic utilitarians the good to be maximized is not essentially an aggregate whose parts inhere in individuals; it is rather a corporate good. The question of who should have political power is hence to be answered not by aggregating individual decisions but rather by reference to this ultimate good. In Rousseau, it is the "general will," which is not necessarily identical with the "will of all," that determines this; and the "general will" refers more to the ideal common interest than to the majority vote although, as we have seen, each individual is equally a part of the general will, and in practice the majority should decide—but only if it contains the qualities of the general will. In Hegel, on the other hand, such egalitarian considerations are omitted; it is the spirit of the nation, as reflected in its historical development, which determines who should rule.

In practice, the organic utilitarians are often close to the status deontologists, and the individualist utilitarians are close to the consent-deontologists. Most of the latter upheld some form of liberal democracy, while most of the former upheld some form of absolutism. The premisses, however, were different, so that if we look at the logic of their arguments, what their premisses logically entitled them to defend and attack, we can see some important potential differences in practice.

VII. WHAT SHOULD BE THE LIMITS OF POLITICAL POWER?

The source or locus of political power may also be viewed as its limit: political power should be limited to those who have the right to exercise it. There still remains, however, the distinct question of what limits there should be on political power regardless of who has or exercises it. This vitally important problem has two parts: (a) What should be the limits as to the *procedures* or *operations* of government? (b) What should be the limits as to the range of *objects* or *acts* controlled by government? This latter part is the problem of what rights or freedoms of individuals must be kept independent of any governmental control, and it is also close to the problem of what rights the individual has against the state.

Political philosophers have sought to present the criteria of such limits in two distinct ways. One way is formal-deontological. This way specifies the moral limits of political power by reference to certain logical-relational requirements. The requirement as to the *procedures* of political power is of the kind called by Aristotle the "rule of law" and by Rousseau the "essence of the general will." The key idea here is that of universality or generality. Political power must operate through laws, and laws are distinct from "decrees" in that they are general regulations applying to whole classes of acts or situations, and to all men equally, including the lawmakers themselves, insofar as they fall under the general specifications stated in the laws. In this sense, laws are "principled"; they apply the same principle to all similar cases demarcated by the law.

The trouble with this formal principle was already pointed out by Aristotle, who wrote that laws themselves may be "unjust." By this he meant that laws may be general in the sense indicated and yet discriminate against one group in favor of another. For law involves classification, and classes of "similar" persons may be singled out for similar treatment on grounds that have nothing to do with their relative merits.

The formal requirement of the limits of political power as these concern the range of *objects* or *acts* which political power ought not to control is presented in the principle of "equal freedom." This holds that a man should be free to do any act if his doing it leaves other men equally free. This general principle has received several distinct interpretations. One interpretation iṣ that of reciprocal acceptability or willingness: a man should be free to do any act to another if he is willing that the other do the same kind of act to him. A second interpretation is that of the possibility of reciprocal action with no specific reference to the agent's reciprocal willingness: a man should be free to do any act to another if his doing it leaves that other free to do the same kind of act to him. A third interpretation is that of the maintenance of general freedom: a man should be free to do any act to another so long as his doing it does not diminish that other's general freedom of action. The first of these interpretations is found in Hobbes, Hume, and Rousseau; the second, in Herbert Spencer; the third, in Kant.

The difficulty with the principle of equal freedom is similar to that which we saw in the principle of universality. Acts may satisfy the conditions of the principle and yet be patently unjust or otherwise morally wrong. The reason for this is that equality or reciprocity, being a purely formal relation, does not specify anything about the nature of the relata, the acts or objects which are equalized. Thus, according to the first interpretation of the principle of equal freedom, A should be free to assault B if A is willing that B assault A. According to the second interpretation of the principle, A should be free to assault B so long as this leaves B free to assault A. According to the third interpretation, a man should be free to dispose of his garbage in any way he likes, or to refrain from paying taxes for schools or post-office, since his doing so does not diminish the general freedom of others.

These difficulties of the formal criteria have led other political philosophers to set forth various material or substantive criteria of the moral limits of political power. Like the formal criteria, the material ones concern the procedures and the objects of political power. One type of such procedural limit is, of course, that of the democratic process itself, with its provisions for the consent of the governed, and hence for the responsibility of the governors to the governed. Since, however, the problem of the limits of political power applies even to democratic power, it seems that these limits must in good part refer to the objects rather than to the procedures of power.

Let us consider a utilitarian material criterion of what should be the objects or acts free from governmental control. This criterion is close to, but not identical with, the varieties of the principle of equal freedom discussed above. It specifies the area of freedom not by formal relations of reciprocity or generality but by the material condition of the nonharmfulness of the acts. According to this, which I shall call the *negative utilitarian* interpretation of the principle, a man should be free to do any act so long as his doing it does not harm anyone else. This does not entail, of course, that every harmful act *should* be prohibited by government. As J. S. Mill points out, many kinds of competitive situations are harmful to the loser and yet beneficial to society. Mill concludes that government should prohibit only those harmful acts where the means employed are themselves harmful to society, namely, force and fraud.

This negative utilitarian interpretation incurs at least two difficulties. One is that there may be serious disagreement as to what is harmful, as is shown, for example, by the many discussions of pornography. The other is that an act may not be harmful in itself, and yet the public good may be advanced by controlling or restricting it. An example would be where someone owns property in an area needed for building a new public school. This latter difficulty involves the perennial problem of the relation between the individual's rights and the public interest. Although Mill declares that he does not base his argument for liberty on "abstract right, as a thing independent of utility," and says that he regards "utility as the ultimate appeal on all ethical questions," his definition of utility is very close to one of the main traditions of natural rights, as found, for example, in Locke. Thus Mill writes that "it must be utility in the largest sense, grounded on the permanent interests of a man as a progressive being." Despite Locke's fame as an upholder of natural rights, he too suggests, like Mill, that those rights are not "absolute"; they are all limited by the public good. Essentially the same utilitarian position is found not only in Bentham but also in the natural-law doctrine of Thomas Aquinas. This position is hence close to that of the organicists, save that the latter tend to view the limit in positive rather than negative terms, such that government is justified in restricting individual freedom wherever this can advance the general social good and not merely where this is needed to prevent harm.

With respect to such overriding of individual rights by considerations of the public good, however, three distinctions are highly relevant: not only (1) between negative and positive utilitarianism, but also (2) between different degrees of importance of goods and rights, and (3) between just and unjust losses of rights. It is one thing, for example, to say that individual rights may be overridden by any increase of public good (positive utilitarianism) and it is another thing to say that they may be overridden in order to avoid some serious public evil (negative utilitarianism). Moreover if there is to be a justified connection between one or more persons' losing a right and the avoidance of some grave public evil or the gaining of some great public good, then not only must the loss be a necessary condition of the avoidance or the gain, but the allocation of the losers must be made impartially.

VIII. WHAT SHOULD BE THE ENDS OF POLITICAL POWER?

Considerations about ends figured prominently in all the other basic questions discussed above, since such considerations are, of course, central to utilitarianism. Nevertheless, the question of ends is distinct from all ·the other questions. In particular, the ends of political power are not the same as its limits. The limits are what government ought not to do, the boundaries beyond which it should not extend; but the ends are what government ought to do, the desirable purposes it should aim to fulfill. The ends, then, cannot be inferred from the limits.

The utilitarians, both individualist and organicist, answer the question what should be the ends of political power by reference to the maximizing of goods, individual or collective. Hence the principle of their answer to the question of ends is the same as that of their answer to the question of limits: government ought to act where this will do more good than harm, and it must refrain from acting where this will do more harm than good. For the organicists, of course, good and harm are assayed in terms of the social whole as a distinct entity, while for the individualists good and harm are assayed in terms of aggregates of individuals. There are also other important differences as to the criteria of "good" and "harm." We may get at some of them by noting that this question of ends involves an important deontological dimension: that of the just distribution of goods. Here we may distinguish two main positions, parallel to the distinction between formal and material conceptions of justice referred to in Section V. One position is closely related to that of the natural-rights deontologists. It holds that the criterion of a just distribution is that it shall have been the consequence of, or at least shall have been regulated by, the legal framework itself. So long as that framework is maintained, with its impartial rules providing for equal freedom to pursue one's interests and for enforcement of contracts, each person will get what his intelligence and industry entitle him to have. The end of government, then, is largely restricted to maintaining this framework. This is the school of those called "liberals" in the nineteenth century and "conservatives" in the twentieth.

The other deontological position is more related to the organicists. It holds that men are so closely tied to their social context that it is impossible in any very direct way to specify what it is just for each individual to have as a function solely of his own efforts or intelligence. The effort and intelligence which an individual displays are themselves in important part the result of social forces. Hence the problem of distributive justice is tied to a more positive view of the end of government. Government must act not merely to preserve an impartial legal order which "interferes" with individual action as little as possible; it must also bring positive action to bear both to protect each person in an important degree from evils like physical disease and economic privation and to promote the conditions which foster equality of opportunity for each individual. These are the twentieth-century variety of "liberals" and exponents of the "welfare state," but their ancestry can be seen not only in modern organicists like Rousseau, Hegel, and Marx but also in such older ones as Plato, Aristotle, and Aquinas. It is at once paradoxical and significant, however, that whereas many of the organicists used the fact of the determination of individual traits by the social context to "justify" a conservative adherence to historical continuities, present-day liberals use the same fact to "justify" energetic governmental intervention in order to change such continuities. Obviously, then, more than the facts alone enter into the respective justifications. The significant advance made in recent times consists in fusing the organicists' emphasis on social determination and social service with the individualists' emphasis on equality of opportunity and free development of the individual.

We have now concluded our brief, schematic consideration of moral criteria that have been applied in answering the basic questions of political philosophy. Because of the nature both of the questions themselves and of the criteria applied to them, there may be important conflicts among the answers, even in those thinkers who uphold what seems like a single, uniform position, such as that of liberal democracy. This becomes especially clear if we restrict ourselves to the three specific questions about political power. For example, a government which is democratic in the sense of operating by majority consent (first question) may not always respect minority rights (second question); and a welfare government (third question) need not be either democratic or constitutionally liberal. The political problem of the twentieth century is in important part that of achieving for all men government that is at once democratic, constitutionally liberal, and concerned with equality of opportunity for individual development and with social welfare. I think that the potential conflicts among these various elements can to a large extent be avoided if the deontological and utilitarian criteria sketched above are properly interpreted and interrelated. The theoretical and practical importance of this task is a decisive reason for inviting the student to participate in the continuing and perennial enterprise of political philosophy.

THOMAS HOBBES

Infinite Desire and Absolute Government

Thomas Hobbes was born in Malmesbury in 1588, the year of the Spanish Armada when, as he wrote, "my mother bore twins, myself and fear." He was educated at Magdalen College, Oxford, whose "Aristotelian" curriculum he always disparaged. He became tutor to the younger son of the Earl of Cavendish and was tutor to the future Charles II in Paris after 1646. Leviathan was published in 1651 while Hobbes was there as a refugee from the Civil War. In 1661 he returned to England, where he died in 1670. His other chief works were De Corpore (*Concerning Body*), De Homine (*Concerning Man*), De Cive (*Concerning the Citizen*), Elements of Law, *and* Behemoth.

[THE INFINITY OF HUMAN DESIRE][1]

Continuall successe, in obtaining those things which a man from time to time desireth, that is to say, continuall prospering, is that men call FELICITY; I mean the Felicity of this life. For there is no such thing as perpetuall Tranquillity of mind, while we live here; because Life it selfe is but Motion, and can never be without Desire, nor without Feare, no more than without Sense. What kind of Felicity God hath ordained to them that devoutly honour him, a man shall no sooner know, than enjoy; being joyes, that now are as incomprehensible, as the word of Schoole-men *Beatificall Vision* is unintelligible. . . .

. . . the Felicity of this life, consisteth not in the repose of a mind satisfied. For there is no such *Finis ultimus,* (utmost ayme,) nor *Summum Bonum,* (greatest Good,) as is spoken of in the Books of the old Morall Philosophers. Nor can a man any more live, whose Desires are at an end, than he, whose Senses and Imaginations are at a stand. Felicity is a continuall progresse of the desire, from one object to another; the attaining of the former, being still but the way to the later. The cause whereof is, That the object of mans desire, is not to enjoy once onely, and for one instant of time; but to assure for ever, the way of his future desire. And therefore the vol-

Selections from *Leviathan.*

[1] From Chapters VI and XI.

31

untary actions, and inclinations of all men, tend, not onely to the procuring, but also the assuring of a contented life; and differ onely in the way; which ariseth partly from the diversity of passions, in divers men; and partly from the difference of the knowledge, or opinion each one has of the causes, which produce the effect desired.

So that in the first place, I put for a generall inclination of all mankind, a perpetuall and restlesse desire of Power after power, that ceaseth onely in Death. And the cause of this, is not alwayes that a man hopes for a more intensive delight, than he has already attained to; or that he cannot be content with a moderate power: but because he cannot assure the power and means to live well, which he hath present, without the acquisition of more. And from hence it is, that Kings, whose power is greatest, turn their endeavours to the assuring it at home by Lawes, or abroad by Wars: and when that is done, there succeedeth a new desire; in some, of Fame from new Conquest; in others, of ease and sensuall pleasure; in others, of admiration, or being flattered for excellence in some art, or other ability of the mind. . . .

OF THE NATURAL CONDITION OF MANKIND, AS CONCERNING THEIR FELICITY, AND MISERY [2]

Nature hath made men so equall, in the faculties of body, and mind; as that though there bee found one man sometimes manifestly stronger in body, or of quicker mind then another; yet when all is reckoned together, the difference between man, and man, is not so considerable, as that one man can thereupon claim to himselfe any benefit, to which another may not pretend, as well as he. For as to the strength of body, the weakest has strength enough to kill the strongest, either by secret machination, or by confederacy with others, that are in the same danger with himselfe.

And as to the faculties of the mind, (setting aside the arts grounded upon words, and especially that skill of proceeding upon generall, and infallible rules, called Science; which very few have, and but in few things; as being not a native faculty, born with us; nor attained, (as Prudence,) while we look after somewhat els,) I find yet a greater equality amongst men, than that of strength. For Prudence, is but Experience; which equall time, equally bestowes on all men, in those things they equally apply themselves unto. That which may

[2] Chapter XIII.

perhaps make such equality incredible, is but a vain conceipt of ones owne wisdome, which almost all men think they have in a greater degree, than the Vulgar; that is, than all men but them-selves, and a few others, whom by Fame, or for concurring with themselves, they approve. For such is the nature of men, that howso-ever they may acknowledge many others to be more witty, or more eloquent, or more learned; Yet they will hardly believe there be many so wise as themselves: For they see their own wit at hand, and other mens at a distance. But this proveth rather that men are in that point equall, than unequall. For there is not ordinarily a greater signe of the equall distribution of any thing, than that every man is contented with his share.

From this equality of ability, ariseth equality of nope in the at-taining of our Ends. And therefore if any two men desire the same thing, which neverthelesse they cannot both enjoy, they become enemies; and in the way to their End, (which is principally their owne conservation, and sometimes their delectation only,) endeav-our to destroy, or subdue one an other. And from hence it comes to passe, that where an Invader hath no more to feare, than an other mans single powor; if one plant, sow, build, or possesse a convenient Seat, others may probably be expected to come prepared with forces united, to dispossesse, and deprive him, not only of the fruit of his labour, but also of his life, or liberty. And the Invader again is in the like danger of another.

And from this diffidence of one another, there is no way for any man to secure himselfe, so reasonable, as Anticipation; that is, by force, or wiles, to master the persons of all men he can, so long, till he see no other power great enough to endanger him: And this is no more than his own conservation requireth, and is generally al-lowed. Also because there be some, that taking pleasure in contem-plating their own power in the acts of conquest, which they pursue farther than their security requires; if others, that otherwise would be glad to be at ease within modest bounds, should not by invasion increase their power, they would not be able, long time, by standing only on their defence, to subsist. And by consequence, such aug-mentation of dominion over men, being necessary to a mans con-servation, it ought to be allowed him.

Againe, men have no pleasure, (but on the contrary a great deale of griefe) in keeping company, where there is no power able to over-awe them all. For every man looketh that his companion should value him, at the same rate he sets upon himselfe: And upon all signes of contempt, or undervaluing, naturally endeavours, as far as he dares (which amongst them that have no common power to keep them in quiet, is far enough to make them destroy each other,) to extort a greater value from his contemners, by dommage; and from others, by the example.

So that in the nature of man, we find three principall causes of quarrell. First, Competition; Secondly, Diffidence; Thirdly, Glory.

The first, maketh men invade for Gain; the second, for Safety; and the third, for Reputation. The first use Violence, to make themselves Masters of other mens persons, wives, children, and cattell; the second, to defend them; the third, for trifles, as a word, a smile, a different opinion, and any other signe of undervalue, either direct in their Persons, or by reflexion in their Kindred, their Friends, their Nation, their Profession, or their Name.

Hereby it is manifest, that during the time men live without a common Power to keep them all in awe, they are in that condition which is called Warre; and such a warre, as is of every man, against every man. For WARRE, consisteth not in Battell onely, or the act of fighting; but in a tract of time, wherein the Will to contend by Battell is sufficiently known: and therefore the notion of *Time,* is to be considered in the nature of Warre; as it is in the nature of Weather. For as the nature of Foule weather, lyeth not in a showre or two of rain; but in an inclination thereto of many dayes together; So the nature of War, consisteth not in actual fighting; but in the known disposition thereto, during all the time there is no assurance to the contrary. All other time is PEACE.

Whatsoever therefore is consequent to a time of Warre, where every man is Enemy to every man; the same is consequent to the time, wherein men live without other security, than what their own strength, and their own invention shall furnish them withall. In such condition, there is no place for Industry; because the fruit thereof is uncertain: and consequently no Culture of the Earth; no Navigation, nor use of the commodities that may be imported by Sea; no commodious Building; no Instruments of moving, and removing such things as require much force; no Knowledge of the face of the Earth; no account of Time; no Arts; no Letters; no Society; and which is worst of all, continuall feare, and danger of violent death; And the life of man, solitary, poore, nasty, brutish, and short.

It may seem strange to some man, that has not well weighed these things; that Nature should thus dissociate, and render men apt to invade, and destroy one another: and he may therefore, not trusting to this Inference, made from the Passions, desire perhaps to have the same confirmed by Experience. Let him therefore consider with himselfe, when taking a journey, he armes himselfe, and seeks to go well accompanied; when going to sleep, he locks his dores; when even in his house he locks his chests; and this when he knows there bee Lawes, and publike Officers, armed, to revenge all injuries shall bee done him; what opinion he has of his fellow subjects, when he rides armed; of his fellow Citizens, when he locks his dores; and of his children, and servants, when he locks his chests. Does he not there as much accuse mankind by his actions, as I do by my words? But neither of us accuse mans nature in it. The Desires, and other Passions of man, are in themselves no Sin. No more are the Actions, that proceed from those Passions, till they know a Law that forbids them: which till Lawes be made they cannot know: nor can any Law be made, till they have agreed upon the Person that shall make it.

It may peradventure be thought, there was never such a time, nor condition of warre as this; and I believe it was never generally so, over all the world: but there are many places, where they live so now. For the savage people in many places of *America,* except the government of small Families, that concord whereof dependeth on naturall lust, have no government at all; and live at this day in that brutish manner, as I said before. Howsoever, it may be perceived what manner of life there would be, where there were no common Power to feare; by the manner of life, which men that have formerly lived under a peacefull government, use to degenerate into, in a civill Warre.

But though there had never been any time, wherein particular men were in a condition of warre one against another; yet in all times, Kings, and Persons of Soveraigne authority, because of their Independency, are in continuall jealousies, and in the state and posture of Gladiators; having their weapons pointing, and their eyes fixed on one another; that is, their Forts, Garrisons, and Guns, upon the Frontiers of their Kingdomes; and continuall Spyes upon their neighbours; which is a posture of War. But because they uphold thereby, the Industry of their Subjects; there does not follow from it, that misery, which accompanies the Liberty of particular men.

To this warre of every man against every man, this also is consequent; that nothing can be Unjust. The notions of Right and Wrong, Justice and Injustice have there no place. Where there is no common Power, there is no Law: where no Law, no Injustice. Force, and Fraud, are in warre, the two Cardinall vertues. Justice, and Injustice are none of the Faculties neither of the Body, nor Mind. If they were, they might be in a man that were alone in the world, as well as his Senses, and Passions. They are Qualities, that relate to men in Society, not in Solitude. It is consequent also to the same condition, that there be no Propriety, no Dominion, no *Mine* and *Thine* distinct; but onely that to be every mans, that he can get; and for so long, as he can keep it. And thus much for the ill condition, which man by meer Nature is actually placed in; though with a possibility to come out of it, consisting partly in the Passions, partly in his Reason.

The Passions that encline men to Peace, are Feare of Death; Desire of such things as are necessary to commodious living; and a Hope by their Industry to obtain them. And Reason suggesteth convenient Articles of Peace, upon which men may be drawn to agreement. These Articles, are they, which otherwise are called the Lawes of Nature: whereof I shall speak more particularly, in the two following Chapters.

OF THE FIRST AND SECOND NATURALL LAWES, AND OF CONTRACTS[3]

The Right of Nature, which Writers commonly call *Jus Naturale*, is the Liberty each man hath, to use his own power, as he will himselfe, for the preservation of his own Nature; that is to say, of his own Life; and consequently, of doing any thing, which in his own Judgement, and Reasons, hee shall conceive to be the aptest means thereunto.

By LIBERTY, is understood, according to the proper signification of the word, the absence of externall Impediments: which Impediments, may oft take away part of a mans power to do what hee would; but cannot hinder him from using the power left him, according as his judgement, and reason shall dictate to him.

A law of nature, (*Lex Naturalis*,) is a Precept, or generall Rule, found out by Reason, by which a man is forbidden to do, that, which is destructive of his life, or taketh away the means of preserving the same; and to omit, that, by which he thinketh it may

---

[3] Chapter XIV, in part.

be best preserved. For though they that speak of this subject, use to confound *Jus,* and *Lex, Right* and *Law;* yet they ought to be distinguished; because RIGHT, consisteth in liberty to do, or to forbeare; Whereas LAW, determineth, and bindeth to one of them: so that Law, and Right, differ as much, as Obligation, and Liberty; which in one and the same matter are inconsistent.

And because the condition of Man, (as hath been declared in the precedent Chapter) is a condition of Warre of every one against every one; in which case every one is governed by his own Reason; and there is nothing he can make use of, that may not be a help unto him, in preserving his life against his enemyes; It followeth, that in such a condition, every man has a Right to every thing; even to one anothers body. And therefore, as long as this naturall Right of every man to every thing endureth, there can be no security to any man, (how strong or wise soever he be,) of living out the time, which Nature ordinarily alloweth men to live. And consequently it is a precept, or generall rule of Reason, *That every man, ought to endeavour Peace, as farre as he has hope of obtaining it; and when he cannot obtain it, that he may seek, and use, all helps, and advantages of Warre.* The first branch of which Rule, containeth the first, and Fundamentall Law of Nature; which is, *to seek Peace, and follow it.* The Second, the summe of the Right of Nature; which is, *By all means we can, to defend our selves.*

From this Fundamentall Law of Nature, by which men are commanded to endeavour Peace, is derived this second Law; *That a man be willing, when others are so too, as farre-forth, as for Peace, and defence of himselfe he shall think it necessary, to lay down this right to all things; and be contented with so much liberty against other men, as he would allow other men against himselfe.* For as long as every man holdeth this Right, of doing any thing he liketh; so long are all men in the condition of Warre. But if other men will not lay down their Right, as well as he; then there is no Reason for any one, to devest himselfe of his: For that were to expose himselfe to Prey, (which no man is bound to) rather than to dispose himselfe to Peace. This is that Law of the Gospell; *Whatsoever you require that others should do to you, that do ye to them.* And that Law of all men, *Quod tibi fieri non vis, alteri ne feceris.* . . .

Whensoever a man Transferreth his Right, or Renounceth it; it is either in consideration of some Right reciprocally transferred to himselfe; or for some other good he hopeth for thereby. For it is a voluntary act: and of the voluntary acts of every man, the object is some *Good to himselfe*. And therefore there be some Rights, which no man can be understood by any words, or other signes, to have abandoned, or transferred. As first a man cannot lay down the right of resisting them, that assault him by force, or take away his life; because he cannot be understood to ayme thereby, at any Good to himselfe. The same may be sayd of Wounds, and Chayns, and Imprisonment; both because there is no benefit consequent to such patience; as there is to the patience of suffering another to be wounded, or imprisoned: as also because a man cannot tell, when he seeth men proceed against him by violence, whether they intend his death or not. And lastly the motive, and end for which this renouncing, and transferring of Right is introduced, is nothing else but the security of a mans person, in his life, and in the means of so preserving life, as not to be weary of it. And therefore if a man by words, or other signes, seem to despoyle himselfe of the End, for which those signes were intended; he is not to be understood as if he meant it, or that it was his will; but that he was ignorant of how such words and actions were to be interpreted.

The mutuall transferring of Right, is that which men call CON-TRACT. . . .

OF THE CAUSES, GENERATION, AND DEFINITION OF A COMMON-WEALTH[4]

The finall Cause, End, or Designe of men, (who naturally love Liberty, and Dominion over others,) in the introduction of that restraint upon themselves, (in which wee see them live in Commonwealths,) is the foresight of their own preservation, and of a more contented live thereby; that is to say, of getting themselves out from that miserable condition of Warre, which is necessarily consequent (as hath been shewn) to the naturall Passions of men, when there is no visible Power to keep them in awe, and tye them by feare of punishment to the performance of their Covenants, and observation of those Lawes of Nature set down in the fourteenth and fifteenth Chapters.

For the Lawes of Nature (as *Justice, Equity, Modesty, Mercy,* and (in summe) *doing to others, as wee would be done to,*) of themselves, without the terrour of some Power, to cause them to be observed, are contrary to our naturall Passions, that carry us to Par-

[4] Chapter XVII, in part.

tiality, Pride, Revenge, and the like. And Covenants, without the Sword, are but Words, and of no strength to secure a man at all. Therefore notwithstanding the Lawes of Nature, (which every one hath then kept, when he has the will to keep them, when he can do it safely,) if there be no Power erected, or not great enough for our security; every man will, and may lawfully rely on his own strength and art, for caution against all other men. . . .

The only way to erect such a Common Power, as may be able to defend them from the invasion of Forraigners, and the injuries of one another, and thereby to secure them in such sort, as that by their owne industrie, and by the fruites of the Earth, they may nourish themselves and live contentedly; is, to conferre all their power and strength upon one Man, or upon one Assembly of men, that may reduce all their Wills, by plurality of voices, unto one Will: which is as much as to say, to appoint one Man, or Assembly of men, to beare their Person; and every one to owne, and acknowledge himselfe to be Author of whatsoever he that so beareth their Person, shall Act, or cause to be Acted, in those things which concerne the Common Peace and Safetie; and therein to submit their Wills, every one to his Will, and their Judgements, to his Judgment. This is more than Consent, or Concord; it is a reall Unitie of them all, in one and the same Person, made by Covenant of every man with every man, in such manner, as if every man should say to every man, *I Authorise and give up my Right of Governing my selfe, to this Man, or to this Assembly of men, on this condition, that thou give up thy Right to him, and Authorise all his Actions in like manner.* This done, the Multitude so united in one Person, is called a COMMON-WEALTH, in latine CIVITAS. This is the Generation of that great LEVIATHAN, or rather (to speake more reverently) of that *Mortal God,* to which wee owe under the *Immortal God,* our peace and defence. For by this Authoritie, given him by every particular man in the Common-Wealth, he hath the use of so much Power and Strength conferred on him, that by terror thereof, he is inabled to forme the wills of them all, to Peace at home, and mutuall ayd against their enemies abroad. And in him consisteth the Essence of the Common-wealth; which (to define it,) is *One Person, of whose Acts a great Multitude, by mutuall Covenants one with another, have made themselves every one the Author, to the end he may use the strength and means of them all, as he shall think expedient, for their Peace and Common Defence.*

And he that carryeth this Person, is called Soveraigne, and said to have *Soveraigne Power;* and every one besides, his Subject.

The attaining to this Soveraigne Power, is by two wayes. One by Naturall force; as when a man maketh his children, to submit themselves, and their children to his government, as being able to destroy them if they refuse; or by Warre subdueth his enemies to his will, giving them their lives on that condition. The other, is when men agree amongst themselves, to submit to some Man, or Assembly of men, voluntarily, on confidence to be protected by him against all others. This later, may be called a Politicall Common-wealth, or Common-wealth by *Institution;* and the former, a Common-wealth by *Acquisition.* And first, I shall speak of a Common-wealth by Institution.

OF THE RIGHTS OF SOVERAIGNES BY INSTITUTION[5]

A *Common-wealth* is said to be *Instituted,* when a *Multitude* of men do Agree, and *Covenant, every one with every one,* that to whatsoever *Man,* or *Assembly of Men,* shall be given by the major part, the *Right* to *Present* the Person of them all, (that is to say, to be their *Representative;*) every one, as well he that *Voted for it,* as he that *Voted against it,* shall *Authorise* all the *Actions* and Judgements, of that Man, or Assembly of men, in the same manner, as if they were his own, to the end, to live peaceably amongst themselves, and be protected against other men.

From this Institution of a Common-wealth are derived all the *Rights,* and *Facultyes* of him, or them, on whom the Soveraigne Power is conferred by the consent of the People assembled.

First, because they Covenant, it is to be understood, they are not obliged by former Covenant to any thing repugnant hereunto. And Consequently they that have already Instituted a Common-wealth, being thereby bound by Covenant, to own the Actions, and Judgements of one, cannot lawfully make a new Covenant, amongst themselves, to be obedient to any other, in any thing whatsoever, without his permission. And therefore, they that are subjects to a Monarch, cannot without his leave cast off Monarchy, and return to the confusion of a disunited Multitude; nor transferre their Person from him that beareth it, to another Man, or other Assembly of men: for they are bound, every man to every man, to Own, and be

⁵ Chapter XVIII, in part.

reputed Author of all, that he that already is their Soveraigne, shall do, and judge fit to be done: so that any one man dissenting, all the rest should break their Covenant made to that man, which is injustice: and they have also every man given the Soveraignty to him that beareth their Person; and therefore if they depose him, they take from him that which is his own, and so again it is injustice. Besides, if he that attempteth to depose his Soveraign, be killed, or punished by him for such attempt, he is author of his own punishment, as being by the Institution, Author of all his Soveraign shall do: And because it is injustice for a man to do any thing, for which he may be punished by his own authority, he is also upon that title, unjust. And whereas some men have pretended for their disobedience to their Soveraign, a new Covenant, made, not with men, but with God; this also is unjust: for there is no Covenant with God, but by mediation of some body that representeth Gods Person; which none doth but Gods Lieutenant, who hath the Soveraignty under God. But this pretence of Covenant with God, is so evident a lye, even in the pretenders own consciences, that it is not onely an act of unjust, but also of a vile, and unmanly disposition.

Secondly, Because the Right of bearing the Person of them all, is given to him they make Soveraigne, by Covenant onely of one to another, and not of him to any of them; there can happen no breach of Covenant on the part of the Soveraigne; and consequently none of his Subjects, by any pretence of forfeiture, can be freed from his Subjection. That he which is made Soveraigne maketh no Covenant with his Subjects before-hand, is manifest; because either he must make it with the whole multitude, as one party to the Covenant, or he must make a severall Covenant with every man. With the whole, as one party, it is impossible; because as yet they are not one Person: and if he make so many severall Covenants as there be men, those Covenants after he hath the Soveraignty are voyd, because what act soever can be pretended by any one of them for breach thereof, is the act both of himselfe, and of all the rest, because done in the Person, and by the Right of every one of them in particular. Besides, if any one, or more of them, pretend a breach of the Covenant made by the Soveraigne at his Institution; and others, or one other of his Subjects, or himselfe alone, pretend there was no such breach, there is in this case, no Judge to decide the controversie: it returns therefore to the Sword again; and every man recovereth the right of Protecting himselfe by his own strength, contrary to the designe they had in the Institution. It is therefore in vain to grant Soveraignty by way of precedent Covenant. The opinion that any Monarch receiveth his Power by Covenant, that is to say on Condition, proceedeth from want of understanding this easie truth, that Covenants being but words, and breath, have no force to oblige, contain, constrain, or protect any man, but what it has from the publique Sword; that is, from the untyed hands of that Man, or Assembly of men that hath the Soveraignty, and whose actions are avouched by them all, and performed by the strength of them all, in him united. But when an Assembly of men is made Soveraigne; then no man imagineth any such Covenant to have past in the Institution; for no man is so dull as to say, for example, the People of *Rome,* made a Covenant with the Romans, to hold the Soveraignty on such or such conditions; which not performed, the Romans might lawfully depose the Roman People. That men see not the reason to be alike in a Monarchy, and in a Popular Government, proceedeth from the ambition of some, that are kinder to the government of an Assembly, whereof they may hope to participate, than of Monarchy, which they despair to enjoy.

Thirdly, because the major part hath by consenting voices declared a Soveraigne; he that dissented must now consent with the rest; that is, be contented to avow all the actions he shall do, or else justly be destroyed by the rest. For if he voluntarily entered into the Congregation of them that were assembled, he sufficiently declared thereby his will (and therefore tacitely covenanted) to stand to what the major part should ordayne: and therefore if he refuse to stand thereto, or make Protestation against any of their Decrees, he does contrary to his Covenant, and therfore unjustly. And whether he be of the Congregation, or not; and whether his consent be asked, or not, he must either submit to their decrees, or be left in the condition of warre he was in before; wherein he might without injustice be destroyed by any man whatsoever.

Fourthly, because every Subject is by this Institution Author of all the Actions, and Judgments of the Soveraigne Instituted; it followes, that whatsoever he doth, it can be no injury to any of his Subjects; nor ought he to be by any of them accused of Injustice. For he that doth any thing by authority from another, doth therein no injury to him by whose authority he acteth: But by this Institution of a Common-wealth, every particular man is Author of all the

Soveraigne doth; and consequently he that complaineth of injury from his Soveraigne, complaineth of that whereof he himselfe is Author; and therefore ought not to accuse any man but himselfe; no nor himselfe of injury; because to do injury to ones selfe, is impossible. It is true that they that have Soveraigne power, may commit Iniquite; but not Injustice, or Injury in the proper signification.

Fiftly, and consequently to that which was sayd last, no man that hath Soveraigne power can justly be put to death, or otherwise in any manner by his Subjects punished. For seeing every Subject is Author of the actions of his Soveraigne; he punisheth another, for the actions committed by himselfe.

And because the End of this Institution, is the Peace and Defence of them all; and whosoever has right to the End, has right to the Means; it belongeth of Right, to whatsoever Man, or Assembly that hath the Soveraignty, to be Judge both of the meanes of Peace and Defence; and also of the hindrances, and disturbances of the same; and to do whatsoever he shall think necessary to be done, both before hand, for the preserving of Peace and Security, by prevention of Discord at home, and Hostility from abroad; and, when Peace and Security are lost, for the recovery of the same. And therefore,

Sixtly, it is annexed to the Soveraignty, to be Judge of what Opinions and Doctrines are averse, and what conducing to Peace; and consequently, on what occasions, how farre, and what, men are to be trusted withall, in speaking to Multitudes of people; and who shall examine the Doctrines of all bookes before they be published. For the Actions of men proceed from their Opinions; and in the well governing of Opinions, consisteth the well governing of mens Actions, in order to their Peace, and Concord. And though in matter of Doctrine, nothing ought to be regarded but the Truth; yet this is not repugnant to regulating of the same by Peace. For Doctrine repugnant to Peace, can no more be True, than Peace and Concord can be against the Law of Nature. It is true, that in a Commonwealth, where by the negligence, or unskilfullnesse of Governours, and Teachers, false Doctrines are by time generally received; the contrary Truths may be generally offensive: Yet the most sudden, and rough busling in of a new Truth, that can be, does never breake the Peace, but only somtimes awake the Warre. For those men that are so remissely governed, that they dare take up Armes, to defend, or introduce an Opinion, are still in Warre; and their condition not Peace, but only a Cessation of Armes for feare of one another; and they live as it were, in the precincts of battaile continually. It belongeth therefore to him that hath the Soveraign Power, to be Judge, or constitute all Judges of Opinions and Doctrines, as a thing necessary to Peace; thereby to prevent Discord and Civill Warre.

Seventhly, is annexed to the Soveraigntie, the whole power of prescribing the Rules, whereby every man may know, what Goods he may enjoy, and what Actions he may doe, without being molested by any of his fellow Subjects: And this is it men call *Propriety.* For before constitution of Soveraign Power (as hath already been shewn) all men had right to all things; which necessarily causeth Warre: and therefore this Proprietie, being necessary to Peace, and depending on Soveraign Power, is the Act of that Power, in order to the publique peace. . . .

But a man may here object, that the Condition of Subjects is very miserable; as being obnoxious to the lusts, and other irregular passions of him, or them that have so unlimited a Power in their hands. And commonly they that live under a Monarch, think it the fault of Monarchy; and they that live under the government of Democracy, or other Soveraign Assembly, attribute all the inconvenience to that forme of Common-wealth; whereas the Power in all formes, if they be perfect enough to protect them, is the same; not considering that the estate of Man can never be without some incommodity or other; and that the greatest, that in any forme of Government can possibly happen to the people in generall, is scarce sensible, in respect of the miseries, and horrible calamities, that accompany a Civill Warre; or that dissolute condition of masterlesse men, without subjection to Lawes, and a coërcive Power to tye their hands from rapine, and revenge: nor considering that the greatest pressure of Soveraign Governours, proceedeth not from any delight, or profit they can expect in the dammage, or weakening of their Subjects, in whose vigor, consisteth their own strength and glory; but in the restiveness of themselves, that unwillingly contributing to their own defence, make it necessary for their Governours to draw from them what they can in time of Peace, that they may have means on any emergent occasion, or sudden need, to resist, or take advantage on their Enemies. For all men are by nature provided of notable multiplying glasses, (that is their Passions and Selfe-love,) through which, every little payment appeareth a great grievance; but are destitute of those prospective glasses, (namely Morall and Civill Science,) to see a farre off the miseries that hang over them, and cannot without such payments be avoyded.

[LIMIT OF POLITICAL OBLIGATION] [6]

The Obligation of Subjects to the Soveraign, is understood to last as long, and no longer, than the power lasteth, by which he is able to protect them. For the right men have by Nature to protect themselves, when none else can protect them, can by no Covenant be relinquished. The Soveraignty is the Soule of the Commonwealth; which once departed from the Body, the members doe no more receive their motion from it. The end of Obedience is Protection; which, wheresoever a man seeth it, either in his own, or in anothers sword, Nature applyeth his obedience to it, and his endeavour to maintain it. And though Soveraignty, in the intention of them that make it, be immortall; yet is it in its own nature, not only subject to violent death, by foreign war; but also through the ignorance, and passions of men, it hath in it, from the very institution, many seeds of a naturall mortality, by Intestine Discord.

[6] From Chapter XXI. On the limit of obligation, see also above, Chapter XIV, page 38.—Ed.

JOHN LOCKE

Natural Rights and Government by Consent

John Locke was born at Wrington, Somersetshire, in 1632 and was educated at Christ Church, Oxford. He was by profession a physician, but the larger part of his life was spent, under the patronage of the Earl of Shaftesbury, on the Board of Trade and in other political positions. Among his political accomplishments was his drafting the constitution for the colony of Carolina, which provided, among other things, for religious toleration. Because of Shaftesbury's involvement in the conspiracy against the Stuarts, Locke fled to Holland in 1683, but returned to England at the time of the "Glorious Revolution," in 1689. His writings earned him the name "the philosopher of the revolution," and revolutionary thinkers both in France and America were deeply influenced by his teachings. Besides the Two Treatises of Government, *others of his works important for political philosophy were* An Essay Concerning Human Understanding, Letters Concerning Toleration, *and* Essays on the Law of Nature. *He died in 1704.*

It is impossible that the rulers now on earth should make any benefit, or derive any the least shadow of authority from that, which is held to be the fountain of all power, *Adam's private dominion and paternal jurisdiction;* so that he that will not give just occasion to think that all government in the world is the product only of force and violence, and that men live together by no other rules but that of beasts, where the strongest carries it, and so lay a foundation for perpetual disorder and mischief, tumult, sedition, and rebellion (things that the followers of that hypothesis so loudly cry out against), must of necessity find out another rise of government, another original of political power, and another way of designing and knowing the persons that have it, than what Sir Robert Filmer hath taught us.

2. To this purpose, I think it may not be amiss, to set down what I take to be political power; that the power of a magistrate over

Selections from *The Second Treatise of Government: An Essay Concerning the True Original, Extent, and End of Civil Government.*

a subject may be distinguished from that of a father over his children, a master over his servant, a husband over his wife, and a lord over his slave. All which distinct powers happening sometimes together in the same man, if he be considered under these different relations, it may help us to distinguish these powers one from another, and show the difference betwixt a ruler of a commonwealth, a father of a family, and a captain of a galley.

3. Political power, then, I take to be a right of making laws with penalties of death, and consequently all less penalties, for the regulating and preserving of property, and of employing the force of the community, in the execution of such laws, and in the defence of the commonwealth from foreign injury; and all this only for the public good.

THE STATE OF NATURE

4. To understand political power aright, and derive it from its original, we must consider, what state all men are naturally in, and that is, a state of perfect freedom to order their actions, and dispose of their possessions and persons, as they think fit, within the bounds of the law of nature, without asking leave, or depending upon the will of any other man.

A state also of equality, wherein all the power and jurisdiction is reciprocal, no one having more than another; there being nothing more evident, than that creatures of the same species and rank, promiscuously born to all the same advantages of nature, and the use of the same faculties, should also be equal one amongst another without subordination or subjection, unless the lord and master of them all should, by any manifest declaration of his will, set one above another, and confer on him, by an evident and clear appointment, an undoubted right to dominion and sovereignty.

5. This equality of men by nature, the judicious Hooker looks upon as so evident in itself, and beyond all question, that he makes it the foundation of that obligation to mutual love amongst men, on which he builds the duties they owe one another, and from whence he derives the great maxims of justice and charity. His words are:

'The like natural inducement hath brought men to know that it is no less their duty, to love others than themselves; for seeing those things which are equal, must needs all have one measure; if I cannot but wish to receive good, even as much at every man's hands, as any man can wish unto his own soul, how should I look to have any part of my desire herein satisfied, unless myself be careful to satisfy the like desire, which is undoubtedly in other men. We all being of one and the same nature; to have any thing offered them repugnant to this desire, must needs in all respects grieve them as much as me; so that if I do harm, I must look to suffer, there being no reason that others should show greater measure of love to me, than they have by me showed unto them; my desire therefore to be loved of my equals in nature, as much as possible may be, imposeth upon me a natural duty of bearing to themward fully the like affection; from which relation of equality between ourselves and them that are as ourselves, what several rules and canons natural reason hath drawn, for direction of life, no man is ignorant.' *Eccl. Pol.*, lib. i.

6. But though this be a state of liberty, yet it is not a state of license: though man in that state have an uncontrollable liberty to dispose of his person or possessions, yet he has not liberty to destroy himself, or so much as any creature in his possession, but where some nobler use than its bare preservation calls for it. The state of nature has a law of nature to govern it, which obliges every one, and reason, which is that law, teaches all mankind, who will but consult it, that being all equal and independent, no one ought to harm another in his life, health, liberty, or possessions: for men being all the workmanship of one omnipotent, and infinitely wise maker; all the servants of one sovereign master, sent into the world by his order, and about his business; they are his property, whose workmanship they are, made to last during his, not one another's pleasure: and being furnished with like faculties, sharing all in one community of nature, there cannot be supposed any such subordination among us, that may authorize us to destroy one another, as if we were made for one another's uses, as the inferior ranks of creatures are for ours. Every one, as he is bound to preserve himself, and not to quit his station wilfully, so by the like reason, when his own preservation comes not in competition, ought he as much as he can to preserve the rest of mankind, and not unless it be to do justice on an offender, take away, or impair the life, or what tends to the preservation of the life, the liberty, health, limb or goods of another. . . .

19. And here we have the plain difference between the state of nature and the state of war, which however some men have con-

founded, are as far distant as a state of peace, good will, mutual assistance, and preservation; and a state of enmity, malice, violence and mutual destruction are one from another. Men living together according to reason without a common superior on earth, with authority to judge between them, are properly in the state of nature. But force, or a declared design of force upon the person of another, where there is no common superior on earth to appeal to for relief, is the state of war; and 'tis the want of such an appeal gives a man the right of war even against an aggressor, though he be in society and a fellow-subject. Thus, a thief whom I cannot harm, but by appeal to the law, for having stolen all that I am worth, I may kill when he sets on me to rob me but of my horse or coat, because the law, which was made for my preservation, where it cannot interpose to secure my life from present force, which if lost is capable of no reparation, permits me my own defence and the right of war, a liberty to kill the aggressor, because the aggressor allows not time to appeal to our common judge, nor the decision of the law, for remedy in a case where the mischief may be irreparable. Want of a common judge with authority puts all men in a state of nature; force without right upon a man's person makes a state of war both where there is, and is not, a common judge.

PROPERTY

27. Though the earth and all inferior creatures be common to all men, yet every man has a *property* in his own *person*. This nobody has any right to but himself. The *labour* of his body and the *work* of his hands, we may say, are properly his. Whatsoever, then, he removes out of the state that nature hath provided and left it in, he hath mixed his labour with it, and joined to it something that is his own, and thereby makes it his property. It being by him removed from the common state nature placed it in, it hath by this labour something annexed to it that excludes the common right of other men. For this labour being the unquestionable property of the labourer, no man but he can have a right to what that is once joined to, at least where there is enough, and as good left in common for others. . . .

31. It will perhaps be objected to this, that if gathering the acorns or other fruits of the earth, etc., makes a right to them, then any one may engross as much as he will. To which I answer,

Not so. The same law of nature that does by this means give us property, does also bound that property too. *God has given us all things richly,* 1 *Tim.* vi. 12. is the voice of reason confirmed by inspiration. But how far has he given it us, *to enjoy?* As much as any one can make use of to any advantage of life before it spoils, so much he may by his labour fix a property in. Whatever is beyond this is more than his share, and belongs to others. Nothing was made by God for man to spoil or destroy. . . .

47. And thus came in the use of money, some lasting thing that men might keep without spoiling, and that, by mutual consent, men would take in exchange for the truly useful but perishable supports of life.

48. And as different degrees of industry were apt to give men possessions in different proportions, so this invention of money gave them the opportunity to continue and enlarge them. . . .

50. But since gold and silver, being little useful to the life of man, in proportion to food, raiment, and carriage, has its value only from the consent of men, whereof labour yet makes in great part the measure, it is plain that men have agreed to disproportionate and unequal possession of the earth, they having by a tacit and voluntary consent found out a way how a man may fairly possess more land than he himself can use the product of, by receiving in exchange for the overplus, gold and silver, which may be hoarded up without injury to anyone, these metals not spoiling or decaying in the hands of the possessor. This partage of things, in an inequality of private possessions, men have made practicable out of the bounds of society, and without compact, only by putting a value on gold and silver and tacitly agreeing in the use of money. For in governments the laws regulate the right of property, and the possession of land is determined by positive constitutions.

[EQUALITY AND REASON]

54. Though I have said above (*Chap.* 2) *That all men by nature are equal,* I cannot be supposed to understand all sorts of *equality:* Age or virtue may give men a just precedency. Excellency of parts and merit may place others above the common level. Birth may subject some, and alliance or benefits others, to pay an observance to those to whom Nature, gratitude, or other respects, may have made it due; and yet all this consists with the equality which all men are in in respect of jurisdiction or dominion one over another, which was the equality I there spoke of as proper to the business in

hand, being that equal right that every man hath to his natural freedom, without being subjected to the will or authority of any other man.

55. Children, I confess, are not born in this full state of equality, though they are born to it. Their parents have a sort of rule and jurisdiction over them when they come into the world, and for some time after, but it is but a temporary one. The bonds of this subjection are like the swaddling clothes they are wrapt up in and supported by in the weakness of their infancy. Age and reason as they grow up loosen them, till at length they drop quite off, and leave a man at his own free disposal. . . .

THE BEGINNING OF POLITICAL SOCIETIES [CONSENT OF THE INDIVIDUAL AND OF THE MAJORITY]

95. Men being, as has been said, by nature all free, equal, and independent, no one can be put out of this estate and subjected to the political power of another without his own consent, which is done by agreeing with other men, to join and unite into a community for their comfortable, safe, and peaceable living, one amongst another, in a secure enjoyment of their properties, and a greater security against any that are not of it. This any number of men may do, because it injures not the freedom of the rest; they are left, as they were, in the liberty of the state of nature. When any number of men have so consented to make one community or government, they are thereby presently incorporated, and make one body politic, wherein the majority have a right to act and conclude the rest.

96. For, when any number of men have, by the consent of every individual, made a community, they have thereby made that community one body, with a power to act as one body, which is only by the will and determination of the majority. For that which acts any community, being only the consent of the individuals of it, and it being one body, must move one way, it is necessary the body should move that way whither the greater force carries it, which is the consent of the majority, or else it is impossible it should act or continue one body, one community, which the consent of every individual that united into it agreed that it should; and so everyone is bound by that consent to be concluded by the majority. And therefore we see that in assemblies empowered

to act by positive laws where no number is set by that positive law which empowers them, the act of the majority passes for the act of the whole, and of course determines as having, by the law of nature and reason, the power of the whole.

97. And thus every man, by consenting with others to make one body politic under one government, puts himself under an obligation to everyone of that society to submit to the determination of the majority, and to be concluded by it; or else this original compact, whereby he with others incorporates into one society, would signify nothing, and be no compact if he be left free and under no other ties than he was in before in the state of nature. For what appearance would there be of any compact? What new engagement if he were no farther tied by any decrees of the society than he himself thought fit and did actually consent to? This would be still as great a liberty as he himself had before his compact, or anyone else in the state of nature hath, who may submit himself and consent to any acts of it if he thinks fit.

98. For if the consent of the majority shall not in reason be received as the act of the whole, and conclude every individual, nothing but the consent of every individual can make any thing to be the act of the whole, which, considering the infirmities of health and avocations of business, which in a number though much less than that of a commonwealth, will necessarily keep many away from the public assembly; and the variety of opinions and contrariety of interests which unavoidably happen in all collections of men, 'tis next impossible ever to be had. And, therefore, if coming into society be upon such terms, it will be only like Cato's coming into the theatre, *tantum ut exiret.* Such a constitution as this would make the mighty *Leviathan* of a shorter duration than the feeblest creatures, and not let it outlast the day it was born in, which cannot be supposed till we can think that rational creatures should desire and constitute societies only to be dissolved. For where the majority cannot conclude the rest, there they cannot act as one body, and consequently will be immediately dissolved again.

99. Whosoever therefore out of a state of nature unite into a community, must be understood to give up all the power necessary to the ends for which they unite into society to the majority of the community, unless they expressly agreed in any number greater than the majority. And this is done by barely agreeing to unite into

one political society, which is all the compact that is, or needs be, between the individuals that enter into or make up a commonwealth. And thus, that which begins and actually constitutes any political society is nothing but the consent of any number of freemen capable of a majority, to unite and incorporate into such a society. And this is that, and that only, which did or could give beginning to any lawful government in the world. . . .

[EXPRESS AND TACIT CONSENT]

119. Every man being, as has been showed, naturally free, and nothing being able to put him into subjection to any earthly power, but only his own consent, it is to be considered what shall be understood to be a sufficient declaration of a man's consent to make him subject to the laws of any government. There is a common distinction of an express and a tacit consent, which will concern our present case. Nobody doubts but an express consent of any man, entering into any society, makes him a perfect member of that society, a subject of that government. The difficulty is, what ought to be looked upon as a tacit consent, and how far it binds, i.e., how far anyone shall be looked on to have consented, and thereby submitted to any government, where he has made no expressions of it at all. And to this I say, that every man that hath any possession or enjoyment of any part of the dominions of any government doth thereby give his tacit consent, and is as far forth obliged to obedience to the laws of that government, during such enjoyment, as any one under it, whether this his possession be of land to him and his heirs for ever, or a lodging only for a week; or whether it be barely travelling freely on the highway; and, in effect, it reaches as far as the very being of anyone within the territories of that government. . . .

THE ENDS OF POLITICAL SOCIETY
AND GOVERNMENT

123. If man in the state of nature be so free as has been said; if he be absolute lord of his own person and possessions; equal to the greatest and subject to nobody, why will he part with his freedom? Why will he give up this empire, and subject himself to the dominion and control of any other power? To which 'tis obvious to answer, that though in the state of nature he hath such a right, yet the enjoyment of it is very uncertain and constantly exposed

to the invasion of others; for all being kings as much as he, every man his equal, and the greater part no strict observers of equity and justice, the enjoyment of the property he has in this state is very unsafe, very unsecure. This makes him willing to quit this condition which, however free, is full of fears and continual dangers; and 'tis not without reason that he seeks out and is willing to join in society with others who are already united, or have a mind to unite for the mutual preservation of their lives, liberties, and estates, which I call by the general name, property.

124. The great and chief end therefore, of men's uniting into commonwealths, and putting themselves under government, is the preservation of their property; to which in the state of nature there are many things wanting.

First, There wants an established, settled, known law, received and allowed by common consent to be the standard of right and wrong, and the common measure to decide all controversies between them. For though the law of nature be plain and intelligible to all rational creatures, yet men, being biased by their interest, as well as ignorant for want of study of it, are not apt to allow of it as a law binding to them in the application of it to their particular cases.

125. *Secondly,* In the state of nature there wants a known and indifferent judge, with authority to determine all differences according to the established law. For everyone in that state being both judge and executioner of the law of nature, men being partial to themselves, passion and revenge is very apt to carry them too far, and with too much heat in their own cases, as well as negligence and unconcernedness, make them too remiss in other men's.

126. *Thirdly,* In the state of nature there often wants power to back and support the sentence when right, and to give it due execution. They who by any injustice offended, will seldom fail where they are able by force to make good their injustice. Such resistance many times makes the punishment dangerous, and frequently destructive to those who attempt it.

127. Thus mankind, notwithstanding all the privileges of the state of nature, being but in an ill condition while they remain in it, are quickly driven into society. Hence it comes to pass, that we seldom find any number of men live any time together in this state. The inconveniences that they are therein exposed to by the irregular and uncertain exercise of the power every man has of

punishing the transgressions of others, make them take sanctuary under the established laws of government, and therein seek the preservation of their property. 'Tis this makes them so willingly give up every one his single power of punishing to be exercised by such alone as shall be appointed to it amongst them, and by such rules as the community, or those authorized by them to that purpose, shall agree on. And in this we have the original right and rise of both the legislative and executive power as well as of the governments and societies themselves. . . .

131. But though men when they enter into society give up the equality, liberty, and executive power they had in the state of nature into the hands of the society, to be so far disposed of by the legislative as the good of the society shall require, yet it being only with an intention in everyone the better to preserve himself, his liberty and property (for no rational creature can be supposed to change his condition with an intention to be worse), the power of the society or legislative constituted by them can never be supposed to extend farther than the common good, but is obliged to secure everyone's property by providing against those three defects above-mentioned that made the state of nature so unsafe and uneasy. And so, whoever has the legislative or supreme power of any commonwealth, is bound to govern by established standing laws, promulgated and known to the people, and not by extemporary decrees, by indifferent and upright judges, who are to decide controversies by those laws; and to employ the force of the community at home only in the execution of such laws, or abroad to prevent or redress foreign injuries and secure the community from inroads. and invasion. And all this to be directed to no other end but the peace, safety, and public good of the people. . . .

THE EXTENT OF THE LEGISLATIVE POWER

134. The great end of men's entering into society being the enjoyment of their properties in peace and safety, and the great instrument and means of that being the laws established in that society, the first and fundamental positive law of all commonwealths is the establishing of the legislative power; as the first and fundamental natural law, which is to govern even the legislative itself, is the preservation of the society, and (as far as will consist with

the public good) of every person in it. This legislative is not only the supreme power of the commonwealth, but sacred and unalterable in the hands where the community have once placed it; nor can any edict of anybody else, in what form soever conceived, or by what power soever backed, have the force and obligation of a law which has not its sanction from that legislative which the public has chosen and appointed; for without this the law could not have that which is absolutely necessary to its being a law, the consent of the society, over whom nobody can have a power to make laws but by their own consent and by authority received from them; and therefore all the obedience, which by the most solemn ties anyone can be obliged to pay, ultimately terminates in this supreme power, and is directed by those laws which it enacts. Nor can any oaths to any foreign power whatsoever, or any domestic subordinate power, discharge any member of the society from his obedience to the legislative, acting pursuant to their trust, nor oblige him to any obedience contrary to the laws so enacted or farther than they do allow, it being ridiculous to imagine one can be tied ultimately to obey any power in the society which is not the supreme.

135. Though the legislative, whether placed in one or more, whether it be always in being or only by intervals, though it be the supreme power in every commonwealth, yet

First, It is not, nor can possibly be, absolutely arbitrary over the lives and fortunes of the people. For it being but the joint power of every member of the society given up to that person or assembly which is legislator, it can be no more than those persons had in a state of nature before they entered into society, and gave it up to the community. For nobody can transfer to another more power than he has in himself, and nobody has an absolute arbitrary power over himself, or over any other, to destroy his own life, or take away the life or property of another. A man, as has been proved, cannot subject himself to the arbitrary power of another; and having, in the state of nature, no arbitrary power over the life, liberty, or possession of another, but only so much as the law of nature gave him for the preservation of himself and the rest of mankind, this is all he doth, or can give up to the commonwealth, and by it to the legislative power, so that the legislative can have no more than this. Their power in the utmost bounds of it is limited to the public good of the society. It is a power that hath no other end but preservation, and therefore can never have a right to destroy, enslave, or designedly to impoverish the subjects; the obligations of the law of nature cease not in society, but only in many cases are drawn closer, and have, by human laws, known penalties annexed to them to enforce their observation. Thus the law of nature stands as an eternal rule to all men, legislators as well as others. The rules that they make for other men's actions must, as well as their own and other men's actions, be conformable to the law of nature, i.e. to the will of God, of which that is a declaration, and the fundamental law of nature being the preservation of mankind, no human sanction can be good or valid against it.

136. *Secondly,* The legislative or supreme authority cannot assume to itself a power to rule by extemporary arbitrary decrees, but is bound to dispense justice and decide the rights of the subject by promulgated standing laws, and known authorized judges. For the law of nature being unwritten, and so nowhere to be found but in the minds of men, they who, through passion or interest, shall miscite or misapply it, cannot so easily be convinced of their mistake where there is no established judge; and so it serves not as it ought, to determine the rights and fence the properties of those that live under it, especially where everyone is judge, interpreter, and executioner of it too, and that in his own case; and he that has right on his side, having ordinarily but his own single strength, hath not force enough to defend himself from injuries or to punish delinquents. To avoid these inconveniencies which disorder men's properties in the state of nature, men unite into societies that they may have the united strength of the whole society to secure and defend their properties, and may have standing rules to bound it by which everyone may know what is his. To this end it is that men give up all their natural power to the society they enter into, and the community put the legislative power into such hands as they think fit, with this trust, that they shall be governed by declared laws, or else their peace, quiet, and property will still be at the same uncertainty as it was in the state of Nature.

137. Absolute arbitrary power, or governing without settled standing laws, can neither of them consist with the ends of society and government, which men would not quit the freedom of the state of nature for, and tie themselves up under, were it not to preserve their lives, liberties, and fortunes, and by stated rules of right and property to secure their peace and quiet. It cannot be supposed that they should intend, had they a power so to do,

to give to any one or more an absolute arbitrary power over their persons and estates, and put a force into the magistrate's hand to execute his unlimited will arbitrarily upon them; this were to put themselves into a worse condition than the state of nature, wherein they had a liberty to defend their right against the injuries of others, and were upon equal terms of force to maintain it, whether invaded by a single man or many in combination. Whereas by supposing they have given up themselves to the absolute arbitrary power and will of a legislator, they have disarmed themselves, and armed him to make a prey of them when he pleases; he being in a much worse condition that is exposed to the arbitrary power of one man who has the command of a hundred thousand than he that is exposed to the arbitrary power of a hundred thousand single men, nobody being secure, that his will who has such a command is better than that of other men, though his force be a hundred times stronger. . . .

138. *Thirdly,* The supreme power cannot take from any man any part of his property without his own consent. For the preservation of property being the end of government, and that for which men enter into society, it necessarily supposes and requires that the people should have property, without which they must be supposed to lose that by entering into society which was the end for which they entered into it; too gross an absurdity for any man to own. Men therefore in society having property, they have such a right to the goods, which by the law of the community are theirs, that nobody hath a right to their substance, or any part of it, from them without their own consent; without this they have no property at all. For I have truly no property in that which another can by right take from me when he pleases against my consent. Hence it is a mistake to think that the supreme or legislative power of any commonwealth can do what it will, and dispose of the estates of the subject arbitrarily, or take any part of them at pleasure. This is not much to be feared in governments where the legislative consists wholly or in part in assemblies which are variable, whose members upon the dissolution of the assembly are subjects under the common laws of their country, equally with the rest. But in governments where the legislative is in one lasting assembly, always in being, or in one man as in absolute monarchies, there is danger still, that they will think themselves to have a distinct interest from the rest of the community, and so will be apt

to increase their own riches and power by taking what they think fit from the people. For a man's property is not at all secure, though there be good and equitable laws to set the bounds of it between him and his fellow-subjects, if he who commands those subjects have power to take from any private man what part he pleases of his property, and use and dispose of it as he thinks good. . . .

140. 'Tis true, governments cannot be supported without great charge, and 'tis fit everyone who enjoys his share of the protection should pay out of his estate his proportion for the maintenance of it. But still it must be with his own consent, i.e. the consent of the majority, giving it either by themselves or their representatives chosen by them; for if anyone shall claim a power to lay and levy taxes on the people by his own authority, and without such consent of the people, he thereby invades the fundamental law of property, and subverts the end of government. For what property have I in that which another may by right take when he pleases himself?

141. *Fourthly,* The legislative cannot transfer the power of making laws to any other hands, for it being but a delegated power from the people, they who have it cannot pass it over to others. The people alone can appoint the form of the commonwealth, which is by constituting the legislative, and appointing in whose hands that shall be. And when the people have said, We will submit, and be governed by laws made by such men, and in such forms, nobody else can say other men shall make laws from them; nor can they be bound by any laws but such as are enacted by those whom they have chosen and authorized to make laws for them. The power of the legislative being derived from the people by a positive voluntary grant and institution, can be no other than what that positive grant conveyed, which being only to make laws, and not to make legislators, the legislative can have no power to transfer their authority of making laws, and place it in other hands. . . .

[THE PEOPLE RETAINS SUPREME POWER]

149. Though in a constituted commonwealth, standing upon its own basis and acting according to its own nature, that is, acting for the preservation of the community, there can be but one supreme power, which is the legislative, to which all the rest are

and must be subordinate, yet the legislative being only a fiduciary power to act for certain ends, there remains still in the people a supreme power to remove or alter the legislative, when they find the legislative act contrary to the trust reposed in them. For all power given with trust for the attaining an end being limited by that end, whenever that end is manifestly neglected or opposed, the trust must necessarily be forfeited, and the power devolve into the hands of those that gave it, who may place it anew where they shall think best for their safety and security. And thus the community perpetually retains a supreme power of saving themselves from the attempts and designs of any body, even of their legislators, whenever they shall be so foolish or so wicked as to lay and carry on designs against the liberties and properties of the subject. For no man or society of men having a power to deliver up their preservation, or consequently the means of it, to the absolute will and arbitrary dominion of another, whenever any one shall go about to bring them into such a slavish condition, they will always have a right to preserve what they have not a power to part with, and to rid themselves of those who invade this fundamental, sacred, and unalterable law of self-preservation, for which they entered into society. And thus the community may be said in this respect to be always the supreme power, but not as considered under any form of government, because this power of the people can never take place till the government be dissolved.

JEAN-JACQUES ROUSSEAU

The Sovereignty of the General Will

Rousseau was born in Geneva in 1712. His mother died in childbirth; his father, first a watchmaker and then a dancing master, gave him an unconventional education. Jean-Jacques ran away from home at the age of sixteen and wandered over Europe. In 1749 he won first prize in an essay contest sponsored by the Academy of Dijon with his reply to the question, "Has the Restoration of the Arts and Sciences Had a Purifying Effect upon Morals?" Rousseau's answer was negative; he said the effect had been corruption. His subsequent works gained him wide attention, and he associated with the leading lights of Paris. He died in poverty in 1778.

Rousseau's most important writings are directly relevant to political philosophy. Besides the Social Contract, *they include the* Discourse on the Origin of Inequality, Discourse on Political Economy, Letters from the Mount, Émile, Project of a Constitution for Corsica, Considerations on the Government of Poland.

BOOK I

I mean to inquire if, in the civil order, there can be any sure and legitimate rule of administration, men being taken as they are and laws as they might be. In this inquiry I shall endeavour always to unite what right sanctions with what is prescribed by interest, in order that justice and utility may in no case be divided. . . .

SUBJECT OF THE FIRST BOOK[1]

Man is born free; and everywhere he is in chains. One thinks himself the master of others, and still remains a greater slave than they. How did this change come about? I do not know. What can make it legitimate? That question I think I can answer. . . .

From the book *The Social Contract and Discourses* by Jean-Jacques Rousseau, trans. G. D. H. Cole, Everyman's Library. Reprinted by permission of E. P. Dutton & Co., Inc., and J. M. Dent & Sons Ltd., London. The excerpts are taken from *The Social Contract*.

[1] From Chapter I.

THE FIRST SOCIETIES [POLITICAL OBLIGATION DOES NOT COME FROM THE FAMILY][2]

The most ancient of all societies, and the only one that is natural, is the family: and even so the children remain attached to the father only so long as they need him for their preservation. As soon as this need ceases, the natural bond is dissolved. The children, released from the obedience they owed to the father, and the father, released from the care he owed his children, return equally to independence. If they remain united, they continue so no longer naturally, but voluntarily; and the family itself is then maintained only by convention.

This common liberty results from the nature of man. His first law is to provide for his own preservation, his first cares are those which he owes to himself; and, as soon as he reaches years of discretion, he is the sole judge of the proper means of preserving himself, and consequently becomes his own master. . . .

THE RIGHT OF THE STRONGEST [POLITICAL OBLIGATION DOES NOT COME FROM FORCE][3]

The strongest is never strong enough to be always the master, unless he transforms strength into right, and obedience into duty. Hence the right of the strongest, which, though to all seeming meant ironically, is really laid down as a fundamental principle. But are we never to have an explanation of this phrase? Force is a physical power, and I fail to see what moral effect it can have. To yield to force is an act of necessity, not of will—at the most, an act of prudence. In what sense can it be a duty?

Suppose for a moment that this so-called "right" exists. I maintain that the sole result is a mass of inexplicable nonsense. For, if force creates right, the effect changes with the cause: every force that is greater than the first succeeds to its right. As soon as it is possible to disobey with impunity, disobedience is legitimate; and, the strongest being always in the right, the only thing that matters is to act so as to become the strongest. But what kind of right is that which perishes when force fails? If we must obey perforce,

[2] From Chapter II.
[3] From Chapter III.

there is no need to obey because we ought; and if we are not forced to obey, we are under no obligation to do so. Clearly, the word "right" adds nothing to force: in this connection, it means absolutely nothing. . . .

Let us then admit that force does not create right, and that we are obliged to obey only legitimate powers. In that case, my original question recurs. . . .

THAT WE MUST ALWAYS GO BACK TO A FIRST CONVENTION[4]

. . . Indeed, if there were no prior convention, where, unless the election were unanimous, would be the obligation on the minority to submit to the choice of the majority? How have a hundred men who wish for a master the right to vote on behalf of ten who do not? The law of majority voting is itself something established by convention, and presupposes unanimity, on one occasion at least.

THE SOCIAL COMPACT[5]

I suppose men to have reached the point at which the obstacles in the way of their preservation in the state of nature show their power of resistance to be greater than the resources at the disposal of each individual for his maintenance in that state. That primitive condition can then subsist no longer; and the human race would perish unless it changed its manner of existence.

But, as men cannot engender new forces, but only unite and direct existing ones, they have no other means of preserving themselves than the formation, by aggregation, of a sum of forces great enough to overcome the resistance. These they have to bring into play by means of a single motive power, and cause to act in concert.

This sum of forces can arise only where several persons come together: but, as the force and liberty of each man are the chief instruments of his self-preservation, how can he pledge them without harming his own interests, and neglecting the care he owes to himself? This difficulty, in its bearing on my present subject, may be stated in the following terms:

"The problem is to find a form of association which will defend and protect with the whole common force the person and goods of each associate, and in which each, while uniting himself with

---

[4] From Chapter V.
[5] Chapter VI.

all, may still obey himself alone, and remain as free as before." This is the fundamental problem of which the *Social Contract* provides the solution.

The clauses of this contract are so determined by the nature of the act that the slightest modification would make them vain and ineffective; so that, although they have perhaps never been formally set forth, they are everywhere the same and everywhere tacitly admitted and recognized, until, on the violation of the social compact, each regains his original rights and resumes his natural liberty, while losing the conventional liberty in favour of which he renounced it.

These clauses, properly understood, may be reduced to one—the total alienation of each associate, together with all his rights, to the whole community. For, in the first place, as each gives himself absolutely, the conditions are the same for all; and, this being so, no one has any interest in making them burdensome to others.

Moreover, the alienation being without reserve, the union is as perfect as it can be, and no associate has anything more to demand: for, if the individuals retained certain rights, as there would be no common superior to decide between them and the public, each, being on one point his own judge, would ask to be so on all; the state of nature would thus continue, and the association would necessarily become inoperative or tyrannical.

Finally, each man, in giving himself to all, gives himself to nobody; and as there is no associate over whom he does not acquire the same right as he yields others over himself, he gains an equivalent for everything he loses, and an increase of force for the preservation of what he has.

If then we discard from the. social compact what is not of its essence, we shall find that it reduces itself to the following terms:

"Each of us puts his person and all his power in common under the supreme direction of the general will, and, in our corporate capacity, we receive each member as an indivisible part of the whole."

At once, in place of the individual personality of each contracting party, this act of association creates a moral and collective body, composed of as many members as the assembly contains voters, and receiving from this act its unity, its common identity, its life, and its will. This public person, so formed by the union of all other persons, formerly took the name of *city,* and now takes that of *Republic* or *body politic;* it is called by its members *State* when passive, *Sovereign* when active, and *Power* when compared with others like itself. Those who are associated in it take collectively the name of *people,* and severally are called *citizens,* as sharing in the sovereign power, and *subjects,* as being under the laws of the State. But these terms are often confused and taken one for another: it is enough to know how to distinguish them when they are being used with precision.

THE SOVEREIGN[6]

This formula shows us that the act of association comprises a mutual undertaking between the public and the individuals, and that each individual, in making a contract, as we may say, with himself, is bound in a double capacity; as a member of the Sovereign he is bound to the individuals, and as a member of the State to the Sovereign. But the maxim of civil right, that no one is bound by undertakings made to himself, does not apply in this case; for there is a great difference between incurring an obligation to yourself and incurring one to a whole of which you form a part.

Attention must further be called to the fact that public deliberation, while competent to bind all the subjects to the Sovereign, because of the two different capacities in which each of them may be regarded, cannot, for the opposite reason, bind the Sovereign to itself; and that it is consequently against the nature of the body politic for the Sovereign to impose on itself a law which it cannot infringe. Being able to regard itself in only one capacity, it is in the position of an individual who makes a contract with himself; and this makes it clear that there neither is nor can be any kind of fundamental law binding on the body of the people—not even the social contract itself. This does not mean that the body politic cannot enter into undertakings with others, provided the contract is not infringed by them; for in relation to what is external to it, it becomes a simple being, an individual.

But the body politic or the Sovereign, drawing its being wholly from the sanctity of the contract, can never bind itself, even to an outsider, to do anything derogatory to the original act, for instance, to alienate any part of itself, or to submit to another Sovereign. Vio-

[6] Chapter VII.

lation of the act by which it exists would be self-annihilation; and that which is itself nothing can create nothing.

As soon as this multitude is so united in one body, it is impossible to offend against one of the members without attacking the body, and still more to offend against the body without the members resenting it. Duty and interest therefore equally oblige the two contracting parties to give each other help; and the same men should seek to combine, in their double capacity, all the advantages dependent upon that capacity.

Again, the Sovereign, being formed wholly of the individuals who compose it, neither has nor can have any interest contrary to theirs; and consequently the sovereign power need give no guarantee to its subjects, because it is impossible for the body to wish to hurt all its members. We shall also see later on that it cannot hurt any in particular. The Sovereign, merely by virrtue of what it is, is always what it should be.

This, however, is not the case with the relation of the subjects to the Sovereign, which, despite the common interest, would have no security that they would fulfil their undertakings, unless it found means to assure itself of their fidelity.

In fact, each individual, as a man, may have a particular will contrary or dissimilar to the general will which he has as a citizen. His particular interest may speak to him quite differently from the common interest: his absolute and naturally independent existence may make him look upon what he owes to the common cause as a gratuitous contribution, the loss of which will do less harm to others than the payment of it is burdensome to himself; and, regarding the moral person which constitutes the State as a *persona ficta,* because not a man, he may wish to enjoy the rights of citizenship without being ready to fulfil the duties of a subject. The continuance of such an injustice could not but prove the undoing of the body politic.

In order then that the social compact may not be an empty formula, it tacitly includes the undertaking, which alone can give force to the rest, that whoever refuses to obey the general will shall be compelled to do so by the whole body. This means nothing less than that he will be forced to be free; for this is the condition which, by giving each citizen to his country, secures him against all personal dependence. In this lies the key to the working of the political machine; this alone legitimizes civil undertakings, which, without it, would be absurd, tyrannical, and liable to the most frightful abuses.

THE CIVIL STATE[7]

The passage from the state of nature to the civil state produces a very remarkable change in man, by substituting justice for instinct in his conduct, and giving his actions the morality they had formerly lacked. Then only, when the voice of duty takes the place of physical impulses and right of appetite, does man, who so far had considered only himself, find that he is forced to act on different principles, and to consult his reason before listening to his inclinations. Although, in this state, he deprives himself of some advantages which he got from nature, he gains in return others so great, his faculties are so stimulated and developed, his ideas so extended, his feelings so ennobled, and his whole soul so uplifted, that, did not the abuses of this new condition often degrade him below that which he left, he would be bound to bless continually the happy moment which took him from it for ever, and, instead of a stupid and unimaginative animal, made him an intelligent being and a man.

Let us draw up the whole account in terms easily commensurable. What man loses by the social contract is his natural liberty and an unlimited right to everything he tries to get and succeeds in getting; what he gains is civil liberty and the proprietorship of all he possesses. If we are to avoid mistake in weighing one against the other, we must clearly distinguish natural liberty, which is bounded only by the strength of the individual, from civil liberty, which is limited by the general will; and possession, which is merely the effect of force or the right of the first occupier, from property, which can be founded only on a positive title.

We might, over and above all this, add, to what man acquires in the civil state, moral liberty, which alone makes him truly master of himself; for the mere impulse of appetite is slavery, while obedience to a law which we prescribe to ourselves is liberty. But I have already said too much on this head, and the philosophical meaning of the word liberty does not now concern us.

REAL PROPERTY[8]

Each member of the community gives himself to it, at the moment of its foundation, just as he is, with all the resources at his command, including the goods he possesses. This act does not make

---

[7] Chapter VIII.
[8] From Chapter IX.

possession, in changing hands, change its nature, and become property in the hands of the Sovereign; but, as the forces of the city are incomparably greater than those of an individual, public possession is also, in fact, stronger and more irrevocable, without being any more legitimate, at any rate from the point of view of foreigners. For the State, in relation to its members, is master of all their goods by the social contract, which, within the State, is the basis of all rights; but, in relation to other powers, it is so only by the right of the first occupier, which it holds from its members. . . .

I shall end this chapter and this book by remarking on a fact on which the whole social system should rest: i.e. that, instead of destroying natural inequality, the fundamental compact substitutes, for such physical inequality as nature may have set up between men, an equality that is moral and legitimate, and that men, who may be unequal in strength or intelligence, become every one equal by convention and legal right.[9]

BOOK II

THAT SOVEREIGNTY IS INALIENABLE[10]

The first and most important deduction from the principles we have so far laid down is that the general will alone can direct the State according to the object for which it was instituted, i.e. the common good: for if the clashing of particular interests made the establishment of societies necessary, the agreement of these very interests made it possible. The common element in these different interests is what forms the social tie; and, were there no point of agreement between them all, no society could exist. It is solely on the basis of this common interest that every society should be governed.

I hold then that Sovereignty, being nothing less than the exercise of the general will, can never be alienated, and that the Sovereign, who is no less than a collective being, cannot be represented except by himself: the power indeed may be transmitted, but not the will.

[9] Under bad governments, this equality is only apparent and illusory; it serves only to keep the pauper in his poverty and the rich man in the position he has usurped. In fact, laws are always of use to those who possess and harmful to those who have nothing: from which it follows that the social state is advantageous to men only when all have something and none too much.

[10] Chapter I.

In reality, if it is not impossible for a particular will to agree on some point with the general will, it is at least impossible for the agreement to be lasting and constant; for the particular will tends, by its very nature, to partiality, while the general will tends to equality. It is even more impossible to have any guarantee of this agreement; for even if it should always exist, it would be the effect not of art, but of chance. The Sovereign may indeed say: "I now will actually what this man wills, or at least what he says he wills"; but it cannot say: "What he wills to-morrow, I too shall will" because it is absurd for the will to bind itself for the future, nor is it incumbent on any will to consent to anything that is not for the good of the being who wills. If then the people promises simply to obey, by that very act it dissolves itself and loses what makes it a people; the moment a master exists, there is no longer a Sovereign, and from that moment the body politic has ceased to exist.

This does not mean that the commands of the rulers cannot pass for general wills, so long as the Sovereign, being free to oppose them, offers no opposition. In such a case, universal silence is taken to imply the consent of the people. This will be explained later on.

THAT SOVEREIGNTY IS INDIVISIBLE [11]

Sovereignty, for the same reason as makes it inalienable, is indivisible; for will either is, or is not, general; [12] it is the will either of the body of the people, or only of a part of it. In the first case, the will, when declared, is an act of Sovereignty and constitutes law: in the second, it is merely a particular will, or act of magistracy—at the most a decree. . . .

WHETHER THE GENERAL WILL IS FALLIBLE [13]

It follows from what has gone before that the general will is always right and tends to the public advantage; but it does not follow that the deliberations of the people are always equally correct. Our will is always for our own good, but we do not always see what that is; the people is never corrupted, but it is often deceived, and on such occasions only does it seem to will what is bad.

[11] From Chapter II.

[12] To be general, a will need not always be unanimous; but every vote must be counted: any exclusion is a breach of generality.

[13] Chapter III.

There is often a great deal of difference between the will of all and the general will; the latter considers only the common interest, while the former takes private interest into account, and is no more than a sum of particular wills: but take away from these same wills the pluses and minuses that cancel one another,[14] and the general will remains as the sum of the differences.

If, when the people, being furnished with adequate information, held its deliberations, the citizens had no communication one with another, the grand total of the small differences would always give the general will, and the decision would always be good. But when factions arise, and partial associations are formed at the expense of the great association, the will of each of these associations becomes general in relation to the State: it may then be said that there are no longer as many votes as there are men, but only as many as there are associations. The differences become less numerous and give a less general result. Lastly, when one of these associations is so great as to prevail over all the rest, the result is no longer a sum of small differences, but a single difference; in this case there is no longer a general will, and the opinion which prevails is purely particular.

It is therefore essential, if the general will is to be able to express itself, that there should be no partial society within the State, and that each citizen should think only his own thoughts: which was indeed the sublime and unique system established by the great Lycurgus. But if there are partial societies, it is best to have as many as possible and to prevent them from being unequal, as was done by Solon, Numa, and Servius. These precautions are the only ones that can guarantee that the general will shall be always enlightened, and that the people shall in no way deceive itself.

THE LIMITS OF THE SOVEREIGN POWER [15]

If the State is a moral person whose life is in the union of its members, and if the most important of its cares is the care for its

[14] "Every interest," says the Marquis d'Argenson, "has different principles. The agreement of two particular interests is formed by opposition to a third." He might have added that the agreement of all interests is formed by opposition to that of each. If there were no different interests, the common interest would be barely felt, as it would encounter no obstacle; all would go on of its own accord, and politics would cease to be an art.

[15] Chapter IV.

own preservation, it must have a universal and compelling force, in order to move and dispose each part as may be most advantageous to the whole. As nature gives each man absolute power over all his members, the social compact gives the body politic absolute power over all its members also; and it is this power which, under the direction of the general will, bears, as I have said, the name of Sovereignty.

But, besides the public person, we have to consider the private persons composing it, whose life and liberty are naturally independent of it. We are bound then to distinguish clearly between the respective rights of the citizens and the Sovereign,[16] and between the duties the former have to fulfil as subjects, and the natural rights they should enjoy as men.

Each man alienates, I admit, by the social compact, only such part of his powers, goods, and liberty as it is important for the community to control; but it must also be granted that the Sovereign is sole judge of what is important.

Every service a citizen can render the State he ought to render as soon as the Sovereign demands it; but the Sovereign, for its part, cannot impose upon its subjects any fetters that are useless to the community, nor can it even wish to do so; for no more by the law of reason than by the law of nature can anything occur without a cause.

The undertakings which bind us to the social body are obligatory only because they are mutual; and their nature is such that in fulfilling them we cannot work for others without working for ourselves. Why is it that the general will is always in the right, and that all continually will the happiness of each one, unless it is because there is not a man who does not think of "each" as meaning him, and consider himself in voting for all? This proves that equality of rights and the idea of justice which such equality creates originate in the preference each man gives to himself, and accordingly in the very nature of man. It proves that the general will, to be really such, must be general in its object as well as its essence; that it must both come from all and apply to all; and that it loses its natural rectitude when it is directed to some particular and deter-

---

[16] Attentive readers, do not, I pray, be in a hurry to charge me with contradicting myself. The terminology made it unavoidable, considering the poverty of the language; but wait and see.

minate object, because in such a case we are judging of something foreign to us, and have no true principle of equity to guide us.

Indeed, as soon as a question of particular fact or right arises on a point not previously regulated by a general convention, the matter becomes contentious. It is a case in which the individuals concerned are one party, and the public the other, but in which I can see neither the law that ought to be followed nor the judge who ought to give the decision. In such a case, it would be absurd to propose to refer the question to an express decision of the general will, which can be only the conclusion reached by one of the parties and in consequence will be, for the other party, merely an external and particular will, inclined on this occasion to injustice and subject to error. Thus, just as a particular will cannot stand for the general will, the general will, in turn, changes its nature, when its object is particular, and, as general, cannot pronounce on a man or a fact. When, for instance, the people of Athens nominated or displaced its rulers, decreed honours to one, and imposed penalties on another, and, by a multitude of particular decrees, exercised all the functions of government indiscriminately, it had in such cases no longer a general will in the strict sense; it was acting no longer as Sovereign, but as magistrate. This will seem contrary to current views; but I must be given time to expound my own.

It should be seen from the foregoing that what makes the will general is less the number of voters than the common interest uniting them; for, under this system, each necessarily submits to the conditions he imposes on others: and this admirable agreement between interest and justice gives to the common deliberations an equitable character which at once vanishes when any particular question is discussed, in the absence of a common interest to unite and identify the ruling of the judge with that of the party.

From whatever side we approach our principle, we reach the same conclusion, that the social compact sets up among the citizens an equality of such a kind, that they all bind themselves to observe the same conditions and should therefore all enjoy the same rights. Thus, from the very nature of the compact, every act of Sovereignty, i.e. every authentic act of the general will, binds or favours all the citizens equally; so that the Sovereign recognizes only the body of the nation, and draws no distinctions between those of whom it is made up. What, then, strictly speaking, is an act of Sovereignty?

It is not a convention between a superior and an inferior, but a convention between the body and each of its members. It is legitimate, because based on the social contract, and equitable, because common to all; useful, because it can have no other object than the general good, and stable, because guaranteed by the public force and the supreme power. So long as the subjects have to submit only to conventions of this sort, they obey no one but their own will; and to ask how far the respective rights of the Sovereign and the citizens extend, is to ask up to what point the latter can enter into undertakings with themselves, each with all, and all with each.

We can see from this that the sovereign power, absolute, sacred, and inviolable as it is, does not and cannot exceed the limits of general conventions, and that every man may dispose at will of such goods and liberty as these conventions leave him; so that the Sovereign never has a right to lay more charges on one subject than on another, because, in that case, the question becomes particular, and ceases to be within its competency.

When these distinctions have once been admitted, it is seen to be so untrue that there is, in the social contract, any real renunciation on the part of the individuals, that the position in which they find themselves as a result of the contract is really preferable to that in which they were before. Instead of a renunciation, they have made an advantageous exchange: instead of an uncertain and precarious way of living they have got one that is better and more secure; instead of natural independence they have got liberty, instead of the power to harm others security for themselves, and instead of their strength, which others might overcome, a right which social union makes invincible. Their very life, which they have devoted to the State, is by it constantly protected; and when they risk it in the State's defence, what more are they doing than giving back what they have received from it? What are they doing that they would not do more often and with greater danger in the state of nature, in which they would inevitably have to fight battles at the peril of their lives in defence of that which is the means of their preservation? All have indeed to fight when their country needs them; but then no one has ever to fight for himself. Do we not gain something by running, on behalf of what gives us our security, only some of the risks we should have to run for ourselves, as soon as we lost it?

THE RIGHT OF LIFE AND DEATH[17]

The question is often asked how individuals, having no right to dispose of their own lives, can transfer to the Sovereign a right which they do not possess. The difficulty of answering this question seems to me to lie in its being wrongly stated. Every man has a right to risk his own life in order to preserve it. Has it ever been said that a man who throws himself out of the window to escape from a fire is guilty of suicide? Has such a crime ever been laid to the charge of him who perishes in a storm because, when he went on board, he knew of the danger?

The social treaty has for its end the preservation of the contracting parties. He who wills the end wills the means also, and the means must involve some risks, and even some losses. He who wishes to preserve his life at others' expense should also, when it is necessary, be ready to give it up for their sake. Furthermore, the citizen is no longer the judge of the dangers to which the law desires him to expose himself; and when the prince says to him: "It is expedient for the State that you should die," he ought to die, because it is only on that condition that he has been living in security up to the present, and because his life is no longer a mere bounty of nature, but a gift made conditionally by the State.

The death-penalty inflicted upon criminals may be looked on in much the same light: it is in order that we may not fall victims to an assassin that we consent to die if we ourselves turn assassins. In this treaty, so far from disposing of our own lives, we think only of securing them, and it is not to be assumed that any of the parties then expects to get hanged.

Again, every malefactor, by attacking social rights, becomes on forfeit a rebel and a traitor to his country; by violating its laws he ceases to be a member of it; he even makes war upon it. In such a case the preservation of the State is inconsistent with his own, and one or the other must perish; in putting the guilty to death, we slay not so much the citizen as an enemy. The trial and the judgment are the proofs that he has broken the social treaty, and is in consequence no longer a member of the State. Since, then, he has recognized himself to be such by living there, he must be removed by exile as a violator of the compact, or by death as a public enemy; for such

[17] Chapter V.

an enemy is not a moral person, but merely a man; and in such a case the right of war is to kill the vanquished.

But, it will be said, the condemnation of a criminal is a particular act. I admit it: but such condemnation is not a function of the Sovereign; it is a right the Sovereign can confer without being able itself to exert it. All my ideas are consistent, but I cannot expound them all at once.

We may add that frequent punishments are always a sign of weakness or remissness on the part of the government. There is not a single ill-doer who could not be turned to some good. The State has no right to put to death, even for the sake of making an example, any one whom it can leave alive without danger.

The right of pardoning or exempting the guilty from a penalty imposed by the law and pronounced by the judge belongs only to the authority which is superior to both judge and law, i.e. the Sovereign; even its right in this matter is far from clear, and the cases for exercising it are extremely rare. In a well-governed State, there are few punishments, not because there are many pardons, but because criminals are rare; it is when a State is in decay that the multitude of crimes is a guarantee of impunity. Under the Roman Republic, neither the senate nor the consuls ever attempted to pardon; even the people never did so, though it sometimes revoked its own decision. Frequent pardons mean that crime will soon need them no longer, and no one can help seeing whither that leads. But I feel my heart protesting and restraining my pen; let us leave these questions to the just man who has never offended, and would himself stand in no need of pardon. . . .

BOOK IV

THAT THE GENERAL WILL IS INDESTRUCTIBLE [18]

As long as several men in assembly regard themselves as a single body, they have only a single will which is concerned with their common preservation and general well-being. In this case, all the springs of the State are vigorous and simple and its rules clear and luminous; there are no embroilments or conflicts of interests; the common good is everywhere clearly apparent, and only good sense

[18] Chapter I.

is needed to perceive it. Peace, unity, and equality are the enemies of political subtleties. Men who are upright and simple are difficult to deceive because of their simplicity; lures and ingenious pretexts fail to impose upon them, and they are not even subtle enough to be dupes. When, among the happiest people in the world, bands of peasants are seen regulating affairs of State under an oak, and always acting wisely, can we help scorning the ingenious methods of other nations, which make themselves illustrious and wretched with so much art and mystery?

A State so governed needs very few laws; and, as it becomes necessary to issue new ones, the necessity is universally seen. The first man to propose them merely says what all have already felt, and there is no question of factions or intrigues or eloquence in order to secure the passage into law of what every one has already decided to do, as soon as he is sure that the rest will act with him.

Theorists are led into error because, seeing only States that have been from the beginning wrongly constituted, they are struck by the impossibility of applying such a policy to them. They make great game of all the absurdities a clever rascal or an insinuating speaker might get the people of Paris or London to believe. They do not know that Cromwell would have been put to "the bells" by the people of Berne, and the Duc de Beaufort on the treadmill by the Genevese.

But when the social bond begins to be relaxed and the State to grow weak, when particular interests begin to make themselves felt and the smaller societies to exercise an influence over the larger, the common interest changes and finds opponents: opinion is no longer unanimous; the general will ceases to be the will of all; contradictory views and debates arise; and the best advice is not taken without question.

Finally, when the State, on the eve of ruin, maintains only a vain, illusory, and formal existence, when in every heart the social bond is broken, and the meanest interest brazenly lays hold of the sacred name of "public good," the general will becomes mute: all men, guided by secret motives, no more give their views as citizens than if the State had never been; and iniquitous decrees directed solely to private interest get passed under the name of laws.

Does it follow from this that the general will is exterminated or corrupted? Not at all: it is always constant, unalterable, and pure; but it is subordinated to other wills which encroach upon its sphere.

Each man, in detaching his interest from the common interest, sees clearly that he cannot entirely separate them; but his share in the public mishaps seems to him negligible beside the exclusive good he aims at making his own. Apart from this particular good, he wills the general good in his own interest, as strongly as any one else. Even in selling his vote for money, he does not extinguish in himself the general will, but only eludes it. The fault, he commits is that of changing the state of the question, and answering something different from what he is asked. Instead of saying, by his vote, "It is to the advantage of the State," he says, "It is of advantage to this or that man or party that this or that view should prevail." Thus the law of public order in assemblies is not so much to maintain in them the general will as to secure that the question be always put to it, and the answer always given by it.

I could here set down many reflections on the simple right of voting in every act of Sovereignty—a right which no one can take from the citizens—and also on the right of stating views, making proposals, dividing and discussing, which the government is always most careful to leave solely to its members; but this important subject would need a treatise to itself, and it is impossible to say everything in a single work.

VOTING [19]

It may be seen, from the last chapter, that the way in which general business is managed may give a clear enough indication of the actual state of morals and the health of the body politic. The more concert reigns in the assemblies, that is, the nearer opinion approaches unanimity, the greater is the dominance of the general will. On the other hand, long debates, dissensions, and tumult proclaim the ascendancy of particular interests and the decline of the State.

This seems less clear when two or more orders enter into the constitution, as patricians and plebians did at Rome; for quarrels between these two orders often disturbed the comitia, even in the best days of the Republic. But the exception is rather apparent than real; for then, through the defect that is inherent in the body politic, there were, so to speak, two States in one, and what is not true of the two together is true of either separately. Indeed, even in the most stormy times, the *plebiscita* of the people, when the senate

[19] Chapter II.

did not interfere with them, always went through quietly and by large majorities. The citizens having but one interest, the people had but a single will.

At the other extremity of the circle, unanimity recurs; this is the case when the citizens, having fallen into servitude, have lost both liberty and will. Fear and flattery then change votes into acclamation; deliberation ceases, and only worship or malediction is left. Such was the vile manner in which the senate expressed its views under the emperors. It did so sometimes with absurd precautions. Tacitus observes that, under Otho, the senators, while they heaped curses on Vitellius, contrived at the same time to make a deafening noise, in order that, should he ever become their master, he might not know what each of them had said.

On these various considerations depend the rules by which the methods of counting votes and comparing opinions should be regulated, according as the general will is more or less easy to discover, and the State more or less in its decline.

There is but one law which, from its nature, needs unanimous consent. This is the social compact; for civil association is the most voluntary of all acts. Every man being born free and his own master, no one, under any pretext whatsoever, can make any man subject without his consent. To decide that the son of a slave is born a slave is to decide that he is not born a man.

If then there are opponents when the social compact is made, their opposition does not invalidate the contract, but merely prevents them from being included in it. They are foreigners among citizens. When the State is instituted, residence constitutes consent; to dwell within its territory is to submit to the Sovereign.[20]

Apart from this primitive contract, the vote of the majority always binds all the rest. This follows from the contract itself. But it is asked how a man can be both free and forced to conform to wills that are not his own. How are the opponents at once free and subject to laws they have not agreed to?

I retort that the question is wrongly put. The citizen gives his consent to all the laws, including those which are passed in spite of his opposition, and even those which punish him when he dares to

---

[20] This should of course be understood as applying to a free State; for elsewhere family, goods, lack of a refuge, necessity, or violence may detain a man in a country against his will; and then his dwelling there no longer by itself implies his consent to the contract or to its violation.

break any of them. The constant will of all the members of the State is the general will; by virtue of it they are citizens and free.[21] When in the popular assembly a law is proposed, what the people is asked is not exactly whether it approves or rejects the proposal, but whether it is in conformity with the general will, which is their will. Each man, in giving his vote, states his opinion on that point; and the general will is found by counting votes. When therefore the opinion that is contrary to my own prevails, this proves neither more nor less than that I was mistaken, and that what I thought to be the general will was not so. If my particular opinion had carried the day I should have achieved the opposite of what was my will; and it is in that case that I should not have been free.

This presupposes, indeed, that all the qualities of the general will still reside in the majority: when they cease to do so, whatever side a man may take, liberty is no longer possible.

In my earlier demonstration of how particular wills are substituted for the general will in public deliberation, I have adequately pointed out the practicable methods of avoiding this abuse; and I shall have more to say of them later on. I have also given the principles for determining the proportional number of votes for declaring that will. A difference of one vote destroys equality; a single opponent destroys unanimity; but between equality and unanimity, there are several grades of unequal division, at each of which this proportion may be fixed in accordance with the condition and the needs of the body politic.

There are two general rules that may serve to regulate this relation. First, the more grave and important the questions discussed, the nearer should the opinion that is to prevail approach unanimity. Secondly, the more the matter in hand calls for speed, the smaller the prescribed difference in the numbers of votes may be allowed to become: where an instant decision has to be reached, a majority of one vote should be enough. The first of these two rules seems more in harmony with the laws, and the second with practical affairs. In any case, it is the combination of them that gives the best proportions for determining the majority necessary.

---

[21] At Genoa, the word "liberty" may be read over the front of the prisons and on the chains of the galley-slaves. This application of the device is good and just. It is indeed only malefactors of all estates who prevent the citizen from being free. In the country in which all such men were in the galleys, the most perfect liberty would be enjoyed.

The Organic State as the Unity of Individual Desires and Universal Reason

---

Hegel was born in Stuttgart in 1770. After studying theology in the University of Tübingen and serving seven years as a tutor in Switzerland and Germany, he became lecturer in philosophy in Jena in 1801. He was promoted to a professorship there in 1805, but the Battle of Jena put a temporary stop to his university career, and for the next ten years he edited a newspaper and directed a high school. He became professor of philosophy in Heidelberg in 1816, and then from 1818 to his death in 1831 he was professor of philosophy in the University of Berlin, where he achieved an enormous influence. Besides his Philosophy of Right, *his chief works bearing upon political philosophy are* Philosophy of Mind (*the third part of his* Encyclopedia of the Philosophical Sciences) *and the* Lectures on the Philosophy of History.

CRITIQUE OF THE CONTRACTUALIST THEORY OF THE STATE

75. . . . It [1] has recently become very fashionable to regard the state as a contract of all with all. Everyone makes a contract with the monarch, so the argument runs, and he again with his subjects. This point of view arises from thinking superficially of a mere unity of different wills. In contract, however, there are two identical wills who are both persons and wish to remain property-owners. Thus contract springs from a person's arbitrary will, an origin which marriage too has in common with contract. But the case is quite different with the state; it does not lie with an individual's arbitrary will to separate himself from the state, because we are already citizens of the state by birth. The rational end of man is life in the state, and if there is no state there, reason at once demands that one be founded. Permission to enter a state or leave it must be given

From Georg W. F. Hegel, *Philosophy of Right*, trans. T. M. Knox (Oxford: Clarendon Press, 1942). Used by permission of the Clarendon Press, Oxford. Subheads have been supplied by the editor.

[1] Addition to para. 75.

by the state; this then is not a matter which depends on an individual's arbitrary will and therefore the state does not rest on contract, for contract presupposes arbitrariness. It is false to maintain that the foundation of the state is something at the option of all its members. It is nearer the truth to say that it is absolutely necessary for every individual to be a citizen. The great advance of the state in modern times is that nowadays all the citizens have one and the same end, an absolute and permanent end; it is no longer open to individuals, as it was in the Middle Ages, to make private stipulations in connexion with it. . . .

CIVIL SOCIETY: THE ECONOMIC AND LEGAL ORDER (THE "STATE" AS SUPERFICIALLY UNDERSTOOD) IN WHICH EACH INDIVIDUAL PURSUES HIS SELFISH ENDS AND YET COMES UNDER A GENERAL SYSTEM

182. The concrete person, who is himself the object of his particular aims, is, as a totality of wants and a mixture of caprice and physical necessity, one principle of civil society. But the particular person is essentially so related to other particular persons that each establishes himself and finds satisfaction by means of the others, and at the same time purely and simply by means of the form of universality, the second principle here.

183. In the course of the actual attainment of selfish ends—an attainment conditioned in this way by universality—there is formed a system of complete interdependence, wherein the livelihood, happiness, and legal status of one man is interwoven with the livelihood, happiness, and rights of all. On this system, individual happiness, etc., depend, and only in this connected system are they actualized and secured. This system may be prima facie regarded as the external state, the state based on need, the state as the Understanding envisages it. . . .

187. Individuals in their capacity as burghers in this state are private persons whose end is their own interest. This end is *mediated* through the universal which thus *appears* as a *means* to its realization. Consequently, individuals can attain their ends only in so far as they themselves determine their knowing, willing, and acting in a universal way and make themselves links in this chain of social connexions. In these circumstances, the interest of the

Idea—an interest of which these members of civil society are as such unconscious—lies in the process whereby their singularity and their natural condition are raised, as a result of the necessities imposed by nature as well as of arbitrary needs, to formal freedom and formal universality of knowing and willing—the process whereby their particularity is educated up to subjectivity.

188. Civil society contains three moments:

(A) The mediation of need and one man's satisfaction through his work and the satisfaction of the needs of all others—the *System of Needs.*

(B) The actuality of the universal principle of freedom therein contained—the protection of property through the *Administration of Justice.*

(C) Provision against contingencies still lurking in systems (A) and (B), and care for particular interests as a common interest, by means of the *Police* and the *Corporation.* . . .

THE STATE: THE SUPREME ETHICAL ORDER WHICH IS AN END IN ITSELF AND THE CONDITION OF THE INDIVIDUAL'S REALITY AND FREEDOM

258. The state is absolutely rational inasmuch as it is the actuality of the substantial will which it possesses in the particular self-consciousness once that consciousness has been raised to consciousness of its universality. This substantial unity is an absolute unmoved end in itself, in which freedom comes into its supreme right. On the other hand this final end has supreme right against the individual, whose supreme duty is to be a member of the state.

If the state is confused with civil society, and if its specific end is laid down as the security and protection of property and personal freedom, then the interest of the individuals as such becomes the ultimate end of their association, and it follows that membership of the state is something optional. But the state's relation to the individual is quite different from this. Since the state is mind objectified, it is only as one of its members that the individual himself has objectivity, genuine individuality, and an ethical life. Unification pure and simple is the true content and aim of the individual, and the individual's destiny is the living of a universal life. His further particular satisfaction, activity, and mode of conduct have this substantive and universally valid life as their starting point and their result.

259. The Idea of the state
  (a) has immediate actuality and is the individual state as a self-dependent organism—the *Constitution* or *Constitutional Law;*
  (b) passes over into the relation of one state to other states— *International Law;*
  (c) is the universal Idea as a genus and as an absolute power over individual states—the mind which gives itself its actuality in the process of *World-History.*

THE STATE IS A UNITY OF UNIVERSAL END OR PURPOSE AND PARTICULAR INTERESTS

260. The state is the actuality of concrete freedom. But concrete freedom consists in this, that personal individuality and its particular interests not only achieve their complete development and gain explicit recognition for their right (as they do in the sphere of the family and civil society) but, for one thing, they also pass over of their own accord into the interest of the universal, and, for another thing, they know and will the universal; they even recognize it as their own substantive mind; they take it as their end and aim and are active in its pursuit. The result is that the universal does not prevail or achieve completion except along with particular interests and through the co-operation of particular knowing and willing; and individuals likewise do not live as private persons for their own ends alone, but in the very act of willing these they will the universal in the light of the universal, and their activity is consciously aimed at none but the universal end. The principle of modern states has prodigious strength and depth because it allows the principle of subjectivity to progress to its culmination in the extreme of self-subsistent personal particularity, and yet at the same time brings it back to the substantive unity and so maintains this unity in the principle of subjectivity itself.

 . . . In [2] the states of classical antiquity, universality was present, but particularity had not then been released, given free scope, and brought back to universality, i.e. to the universal end of the whole. The essence of the modern state is that the universal be bound up with the complete freedom of its particular members and with private well-being, that thus the interests of family and civil society must concentrate themselves on the state, although the universal

[2] Addition to para. 260.

end cannot be advanced without the personal knowledge and will of its particular members, whose own rights must be maintained. Thus the universal must be furthered, but subjectivity on the other hand must attain its full and living development. It is only when both these moments subsist in their strength that the state can be regarded as articulated and genuinely organized.

261. In contrast with the spheres of private rights and private welfare (the family and civil society), the state is from one point of view an external necessity and their higher authority; its nature is such that their laws and interests are subordinate to it and dependent on it. On the other hand, however, it is the end immanent within them, and its strength lies in the unity of its own universal end and aim with the particular interest of individuals, in the fact that individuals have duties to the state in proportion as they have rights against it.

In [3] the state everything depends on the unity of universal and particular. In the states of antiquity, the subjective end simply coincided with the state's will. In modern times, however, we make claims for private judgement, private willing, and private conscience. The ancients had none of these in the modern sense; the ultimate thing with them was the will of the state. Whereas under the despots of Asia the individual had no inner life and no justification in himself, in the modern world man insists on respect being paid to his inner life. The conjunction of duty and right has a twofold aspect: what the state demands from us as a duty is *eo ipso* our right as individuals, since the state is nothing but the articulation of the concept of freedom. The determinations of the individual will are given an objective embodiment through the state and thereby they attain their truth and their actualization for the first time. The state is the one and only prerequisite of the attainment of particular ends and welfare. . . .

THE CONSTITUTION AS DERIVING FROM THE INHERENT STRUCTURE AND FUNCTIONING OF THE STATE, AS AGAINST SOMETHING EXTERNALLY IMPOSED OR INVENTED

272. The constitution is rational in so far as the state inwardly differentiates and determines its activity in accordance with the na-

[3] Addition to para. 261.

ture of the concept. The result of this is that each of these powers is in itself the totality of the constitution, because each contains the other moments and has them effective in itself, and because the moments, being expressions of the differentiation of the concept, simply abide in their ideality and constitute nothing but a single individual whole.

273. . . . Another question readily presents itself here: 'Who is to frame the constitution?' This question seems clear but closer inspection shows at once that it is meaningless, for it presupposes that there is no constitution there, but only an agglomeration of atomic individuals. How an agglomeration of individuals could acquire a constitution, whether automatically or by someone's aid, whether as a present or by force or by thought, it would have to be allowed to settle for itself, since with an agglomeration the concept has nothing to do. But if the question presupposes an already existent constitution, then it is not about framing, but only about altering the constitution, and the very presupposition of a constitution directly implies that its alteration may come about only by constitutional means. In any case, however, it is absolutely essential that the constitution should not be regarded as something made, even though it has come into being in time. It must be treated rather as something simply existent in and by itself, as divine therefore, and constant, and so as exalted above the sphere of things that are made. . . .

ON POPULAR SOVEREIGNTY

279. . . . The usual sense in which men have recently begun to speak of the 'sovereignty of the people' is that it is something opposed to the sovereignty existent in the monarch. So opposed to the sovereignty of the monarch, the sovereignty of the people is one of the confused notions based on the wild idea of the 'people'. Taken without its monarch and the articulation of the whole which is the indispensable and direct concomitant of monarchy, the people is a formless mass and no longer a state. It lacks every one of those determinate characteristics—sovereignty, government, judges, magistrates, class-divisions, etc.,—which are to be found only in a whole which is inwardly organized. By the very emergence into a people's life of moments of this kind which have a bearing on an organization, on political life, a people ceases to be that indeterminate abstraction which, when represented in a general way, is called the 'people'. . . .

281. . . . An elective monarchy seems of course to be the most natural idea, i.e. the idea which superficial thinking finds handiest. Because it is the concerns and interests of his people for which a monarch has to provide, so the argument runs, it must be left to the people to entrust with its welfare whomsoever it pleases, and only with the grant of this trust does his right to rule arise. This view, like the notion of the monarch as the highest executive official in the state, or the notion of a contractual relation between him and his people, etc., etc., is grounded on the will interpreted as the whim, opinion, and caprice of the Many. A will of this character counts as the first thing in civil society (as was pointed out long ago) or rather it tries to count as the only thing there, but it is not the guiding principle of the family, still less of the state, and in short it stands opposed to the Idea of ethical life. . . .

301. Current opinion has put into general circulation such a host of perverse and false ideas and ways of speaking about 'People', 'Constitution', and 'Estates' that it would be a waste of energy to try to specify, expound, and correct them. The idea uppermost in men's minds when they speak about the necessity or the expediency of 'summoning the Estates' is generally something of this sort: (i) The deputies of the people, or even the people themselves, must know best what is in their best interest, and (ii) their will for its promotion is undoubtedly the most disinterested. So far as the first of these points is concerned, however, the truth is that if 'people' means a particular section of the citizens, then it means precisely that section which does *not* know what it wills. To know what one wills, and still more to know what the absolute will, Reason, wills, is the fruit of profound apprehension and insight, precisely the things which are *not* popular. . . .

308. . . . To hold that every single person should share in deliberating and deciding on political matters of general concern on the ground that all individuals are members of the state, that its concerns are their concerns, and that it is their right that what is done should be done with their knowledge and volition, is tantamount to a proposal to put the democratic element without any rational form into the organism of the state, although it is only in virtue of the possession of such a form that the state is an organism at all. This idea comes readily to mind because it does not go beyond the abstraction of 'being a member of the state', and it is superficial thinking which clings to abstractions. The rational considera-

tion of a topic, the consciousness of the Idea, is concrete, and to that extent coincides with a genuine practical sense. Such a sense is itself nothing but the sense of rationality or the Idea, though it is not to be confused with mere business routine or the horizon of a restricted sphere. The concrete state is the whole, articulated into its particular groups. The member of a state is a member of such a group, i.e. of a social class, and it is only as characterized in this objective way that he comes under consideration when we are dealing with the state. His mere character as universal implies that he is at one and the same time both a private person and also a thinking consciousness, a will which wills the universal. This consciousness and will, however, lose their emptiness and acquire a content and a living actuality only when they are filled with particularity, and particularity means determinacy as particular and a particular class-status; or, to put the matter otherwise, abstract individuality is a generic essence, but has its immanent universal actuality as the generic essence next higher in the scale. Hence the single person attains his actual and living destiny for universality only when he becomes a member of a Corporation, a society, etc., and thereby it becomes open to him, on the strength of his skill, to enter any class for which he is qualified, the class of civil servants included.

Another presupposition of the idea that all should participate in the business of the state is that everyone is at home in this business —a ridiculous notion, however commonly we may hear it sponsored. Still, in public opinion a field is open to everyone where he can express his purely personal political opinions and make them count. . . .

PUBLIC OPINION AND FREEDOM OF EXPRESSION

316. The formal subjective freedom of individuals consists in their having and expressing their own private judgements, opinions, and recommendations on affairs of state. This freedom is collectively manifested as what is called 'public opinion', in which what is absolutely universal, the substantive and the true, is linked with its opposite, the purely particular and private opinions of the Many. Public opinion as it exists is thus a standing self-contradiction, knowledge as appearance, the essential just as directly present as the inessential.

317. Public opinion, therefore, is a repository not only of the genuine needs and correct tendencies of common life, but also, in the form of common sense (i.e. all-pervasive fundamental ethical princi-

ples disguised as prejudices), of the eternal, substantive principles of justice, the true content and result of legislation, the whole constitution, and the general position of the state. At the same time, when this inner truth emerges into consciousness and, embodied in general maxims, enters representative thinking—whether it be there on its own account or in support of concrete arguments about felt wants, public affairs, the organization of the state, and relations of parties within it—it becomes infected by all the accidents of opinion, by its ignorance and perversity, by its mistakes and falsity of judgement. Since in considering such opinion we have to do with the consciousness of an insight and conviction peculiarly one's own, the more peculiarly one's own an opinion may be the worse its content is, because the bad is that which is wholly private and personal in its content; the rational, on the other hand, is the absolutely universal, while it is on peculiarity that opining prides itself. . . .

319. Freedom of public communication—of the two modes of communication, the press and the spoken word, the first exceeds the second in range of contact but lags behind it in vivacity—satisfaction of the goading desire to say one's say and to have said it, is directly assured by the laws and by-laws which control or punish its excesses. But it is assured indirectly by the innocuous character which it acquires as a result principally of the rationality of the constitution, the stability of government, and secondly of the publicity of Estates Assemblies. The reason why the latter makes free speech harmless is that what is voiced in these Assemblies is a sound and mature insight into the concerns of the state, with the result that members of the general public are left with nothing of much importance to say, and above all are deprived of the opinion that what they say is of peculiar importance and efficacy. A further safeguard of free speech is the indifference and contempt speedily and necessarily visited on shallow and cantankerous talking.

To define freedom of the press as freedom to say and write whatever we please is parallel to the assertion that freedom as such means freedom to do as we please. Talk of this kind is due to wholly uneducated, crude, and superficial ideas. Moreover, it is in the very nature of the thing that abstract thinking should nowhere be so stubborn, so unintelligent, as in this matter of free speech, because what it is considering is the most fleeting, the most contingent, and the most personal side of opinion in its infinite diversity of content and tergiversation. . . .

ETHICAL SIGNIFICANCE OF WAR. THE INDIVIDUAL'S DUTY TO SACRIFICE HIS LIFE

324. . . . The individual's substantive duty [is] to maintain this substantive individuality, i.e. the independence and sovereignty of the state, at the risk and the sacrifice of property and life, as well as of opinion and everything else naturally comprised in the compass of life.

An entirely distorted account of the demand for this sacrifice results from regarding the state as a mere civil society and from regarding its final end as only the security of individual life and property. This security cannot possibly be obtained by the sacrifice of what is to be secured—on the contrary.

The ethical moment in war is implied in what has been said in this Paragraph. War is not to be regarded as an absolute evil and as a purely external accident, which itself therefore has some accidental cause, be it injustices, the passions of nations or the holders of power, etc., or in short, something or other which ought not to be. It is to what is by nature accidental that accidents happen, and the fate whereby they happen is thus a necessity. Here as elsewhere, the point of view from which things seem pure accidents vanishes if we look at them in the light of the concept and philosophy, because philosophy knows accident for a show and sees in it its essence, necessity. It is necessary that the finite—property and life —should be definitely established as accidental, because accidentality is the concept of the finite. From one point of view this necessity appears in the form of the power of nature, and everything is mortal and transient. But in the ethical substance, the state, nature is robbed of this power, and the necessity is exalted to be the work of freedom, to be something ethical. The transience of the finite becomes a willed passing away, and the negativity lying at the roots of the finite becomes the substantive individuality proper to the ethical substance.

War is the state of affairs which deals in earnest with the vanity of temporal goods and concerns—a vanity at other times a common theme of edifying sermonizing. This is what makes it the moment in which the ideality of the particular attains its right and is actualized. War has the higher significance that by its agency, as I have remarked elsewhere, the ethical health of peoples is preserved in their indifference to the stabilization of finite institutions; just as the blowing of the winds preserves the sea from the foulness which would be the result of a prolonged calm, so also corruption in nations would be the product of prolonged, let alone 'perpetual', peace. This, however, is said to be only a philosophic idea, or, to use another common expression, a 'justification of Providence', and it is maintained that actual wars require some other justification. . . .

WORLD HISTORY

341. The element in which the universal mind exists in art is intuition and imagery, in religion feeling and representative thinking, in philosophy pure freedom of thought. In world history this element is the actuality of mind in its whole compass of internality and externality alike. World history is a court of judgement because in its absolute universality, the particular—i.e. the *Penates*, civil society, and the national minds in their variegated actuality—is present as only ideal, and the movement of mind in this element is the exhibition of that fact.

342. Further, world history is not the verdict of mere might, i.e. the abstract and non-rational inevitability of a blind destiny. On the contrary, since mind is implicitly and actually reason, and reason is explicit to itself in mind as knowledge, world history is the necessary development, out of the concept of mind's freedom alone, of the moments of reason and so of the self-consciousness and freedom of mind. This development is the interpretation and actualization of the universal mind.

KARL MARX AND FRIEDRICH ENGELS

Bourgeois Society: the State as Weapon of the Class Struggle

Marx was born in Trier, Germany, in 1818; Engels in Barmen, Prussia, in 1820. Marx received his doctorate in 1841 from the University of Jena for a dissertation on the philosophies of Democritus and Epicurus. He became editor of a newspaper, which was suppressed in 1843. In 1845 he was expelled from Paris. He edited another newspaper, for which he was indicted for treason in Cologne. On his acquittal he went into exile in England, where he engaged in extensive research and writing at the British Museum. Engels contributed heavily to support Marx and his family, Marx's sole other income being derived from articles written for the New York Tribune. *Marx resumed political activity in 1864 with the founding of the International Workingmen's Association. He died in 1883. Engels continued writing and editing Marx's writings for post-humous publication until his own death in 1895.*

Besides The Communist Manifesto, *Marx and Engels collaborated on* The Holy Family *and* The German Ideology. *Marx's other works include* Capital, Contribution to a Critique of Political Economy, Critique of the Gotha Program, The Poverty of Philosophy, Theses on Feuerbach, The Civil War in France. *Engels' other works include* The Condition of the Working Class in England; The Origin of the Family, Private Property, and the State; Ludwig Feuerbach and the End of Classical German Philosophy; Dialectics of Nature; Anti-Duhring; The Peasant War in Germany.

BOURGEOIS AND PROLETARIANS[1]

The history of all hitherto existing society is the history of class struggles.

Selections from *The Communist Manifesto.* Subheads have been supplied by the editor.

[1] [Note by Engels] By "bourgeoisie" is meant the class of modern capitalists, owners of the means of social production and employers of wage-labor; by "proletariat," the class of modern wage-laborers who, having no means of production of their own, are reduced to selling their labor power in order to live.

[Added note by Ed.] *Bourgeois* is originally a French word meaning "city-dweller" or "town-dweller." *Proletarian* is from the Latin *proletarius,* meaning someone who has no property except his offspring (*proles*). Cf. Cicero, *De re publica,* II. xxii. 40.

Freeman and slave, patrician and plebeian, lord and serf, guild-master and journeyman, in a word, oppressor and oppressed, stood in constant opposition to one another, carried on an uninterrupted, now hidden, now open fight, a fight that each time ended, either in a revolutionary reconstitution of society at large, or in the common ruin of the contending classes.

In the earlier epochs of history, we find almost everywhere a complicated arrangement of society into various orders, a manifold gradation of social rank. In ancient Rome we have patricians, knights, plebeians, slaves; in the Middle Ages, feudal lords, vassals, guild-masters, journeymen, apprentices, serfs; in almost all of these classes, again, subordinate gradations.

The modern bourgeois society that has sprouted from the ruins of feudal society has not done away with class antagonisms. It has but established new classes, new conditions of oppression, new forms of struggle in place of the old ones.

Our epoch, the epoch of the bourgeoisie, possesses, however, this distinctive feature: It has simplified the class antagonisms. Society as a whole is more and more splitting up into two great hostile camps, into two great classes directly facing each other—bourgeoisie and proletariat.

THE RISE OF THE BOURGEOISIE

From the serfs of the Middle Ages sprang the chartered burghers of the earliest towns. From these burgesses the first elements of the bourgeoisie were developed.

The discovery of America, the rounding of the Cape, opened up fresh ground for the rising bourgeoisie. The East-Indian and Chinese markets, the colonization of America, trade with the colonies, the increase in the means of exchange and in commodities generally, gave to commerce, to navigation, to industry, an impulse never before known, and thereby, to the revolutionary element in the tottering feudal society, a rapid development.

The feudal system of industry, in which industrial production was monopolized by closed guilds, now no longer sufficed for the growing wants of the new markets. The manufacturing system took its place. The guild-masters were pushed aside by the manufacturing middle class; division of labor between the different corporate guilds vanished in the face of division of labor in each single workshop.

Meantime the markets kept ever growing, the demand ever rising.

Even manufacture no longer sufficed. Thereupon, steam and machinery revolutionized industrial production. The place of manufacture was taken by the giant, modern industry, the place of the industrial middle class, by industrial millionaires—the leaders of whole industrial armies, the modern bourgeois.

Modern industry has established the world market, for which the discovery of America paved the way. This market has given an immense development to commerce, to navigation, to communication by land. This development has, in its turn, reacted on the extension of industry; and in proportion as industry, commerce, navigation, railways extended, in the same proportion the bourgeoisie developed, increased its capital, and pushed into the background every class handed down from the Middle Ages.

We see, therefore, how the modern bourgeoisie is itself the product of a long course of development, of a series of revolutions in the modes of production and of exchange.

Each step in the development of the bourgeoisie was accompanied by a corresponding political advance of that class. An oppressed class under the sway of the feudal nobility, it became an armed and self-governing association in the medieval commune; here independent urban republic (as in Italy and Germany), there taxable "third estate" of the monarchy (as in France); afterwards, in the period of manufacture proper, serving either the semi-feudal or the absolute monarchy as a counterpoise against the nobility, and, in fact, cornerstone of the great monarchies in general—the bourgeoisie has at last, since the establishment of modern industry and of the world market, conquered for itself, in the modern representative state, exclusive political sway. The executive of the modern state is but a committee for managing the common affairs of the whole bourgeoisie.

REVOLUTIONARY ROLE OF THE BOURGEOISIE

The bourgeoisie has played a most revolutionary role in history.

The bourgeoisie, wherever it has got the upper hand, has put an end to all feudal, patriarchal, idyllic relations. It has pitilessly torn asunder the motley feudal ties that bound man to his "natural superiors," and has left no other bond between man and man than naked self-interest, than callous "cash payment." It has drowned the most heavenly ecstasies of religious fervor, of chivalrous enthusiasm, of philistine sentimentalism, in the icy water of egotistical calculation. It has resolved personal worth into exchange value, and in place of the numberless indefeasible chartered freedoms, has set up that single, unconscionable freedom—Free Trade. In one word, for exploitation, veiled by religious and political illusions, it has substituted naked, shameless, direct, brutal exploitation. . . .

The bourgeoisie cannot exist without constantly revolutionizing the instruments of production, and thereby the relations of production, and with them the whole relations of society. Conservation of the old modes of production in unaltered form, was, on the contrary, the first condition of existence for all earlier industrial classes. Constant revolutionizing of production, uninterrupted disturbance of all social conditions, everlasting uncertainty and agitation distinguish the bourgeois epoch from all earlier ones. All fixed, fast-frozen relations, with their train of ancient and venerable prejudices and opinions, are swept away, all new-formed ones become antiquated before they can ossify. All that is solid melts into air, all that is holy is profaned, and man is at last compelled to face with sober senses his real conditions of life and his relations with his kind. . . .

The bourgeoisie, by the rapid improvement of all instruments of production, by the immensely facilitated means of communication, draws all nations, even the most barbarian, into civilization. The cheap prices of its commodities are the heavy artillery with which it batters down all Chinese walls, with which it forces the barbarians' intensely obstinate hatred of foreigners to capitulate. It compels all nations, on pain of extinction, to adopt the bourgeois mode of production; it compels them to introduce what it calls civilization into their midst, *i.e.*, to become bourgeois themselves. In a word, it creates a world after its own image. . . .

The bourgeoisie, during its rule of scarce one hundred years, has created more massive and more colossal productive forces than have all preceding generations together. Subjection of nature's forces to man, machinery, application of chemistry to industry and agriculture, steam-navigation, railways, electric telegraphs, clearing of whole continents for cultivation, canalization of rivers, whole populations conjured out of the ground—what earlier century had even a presentiment that such productive forces slumbered in the lap of social labor?

THE REVOLT OF PRODUCTIVE FORCES
AGAINST PROPERTY RELATIONS

We see then that the means of production and of exchange, which served as the foundation for the growth of the bourgeoisie, were generated in feudal society. At a certain stage in the development of these means of production and of exchange, the conditions under which feudal society produced and exchanged, the feudal organization of agriculture and manufacturing industry, in a word, the feudal relations of property became no longer compatible with the already developed productive forces; they became so many fetters. They had to be burst asunder; they were burst asunder.

Into their place stepped free competition, accompanied by a social and political constitution adapted to it, and by the economic and political sway of the bourgeois class.

A similar movement is going on before our own eyes. Modern bourgeois society with its relations of production, of exchange and of property, a society that has conjured up such gigantic means of production and of exchange, is like the sorcerer who is no longer able to control the powers of the nether world whom he has called up by his spells. For many a decade past the history of industry and commerce is but the history of the revolt of modern productive forces against modern conditions of production, against the property relations that are the conditions for the existence of the bourgeoisie and of its rule. It is enough to mention the commercial crises that by their periodical return put the existence of the entire bourgeois society on trial, each time more threateningly. In these crises a great part not only of the existing products, but also of the previously created productive forces, are periodically destroyed. In these crises there breaks out an epidemic that, in all earlier epochs, would have seemed an absurdity—the epidemic of overproduction. Society suddenly finds itself put back into a state of momentary barbarism; it appears as if a famine, a universal war of devastation had cut off the supply of every means of subsistence; industry and commerce seem to be destroyed. And why? Because there is too much civilization, too much means of subsistence, too much industry, too much commerce. The productive forces at the disposal of society no longer tend to further the development of the conditions of bourgeois property; on the contrary, they have become too powerful for these conditions, by which they are fettered, and no sooner do they overcome these fetters than they bring disorder into the whole of bourgeois society, endanger the existence of bourgeois property. The conditions of bourgeois society are too narrow to comprise the wealth created by them. And how does the bourgeoisie get over these crises? On the one hand by enforced destruction of a mass of productive forces; on the other, by the conquest of new markets, and by the more thorough exploitation of the old ones. That is to say, by paving the way for more extensive and more destructive crises, and by diminishing the means whereby crises are prevented.

The weapons with which the bourgeoisie felled feudalism to the ground are now turned against the bourgeoisie itself.

THE SLAVERY OF THE PROLETARIAT

But not only has the bourgeoisie forged the weapons that bring death to itself; it has also called into existence the men who are to wield those weapons—the modern working class—the proletarians.

In proportion as the bourgeoisie, *i.e.*, capital, is developed, in the same proportion is the proletariat, the modern working class, developed—a class of laborers, who live only so long as they find work, and who find work only so long as their labor increases capital. These laborers, who must sell themselves piecemeal, are a commodity, like every other article of commerce, and are consequently exposed to all the vicissitudes of competition, to all the fluctuations of the market.

Owing to the extensive use of machinery and to division of labor, the work of the proletarians has lost all individual character, and, consequently, all charm for the workman. He becomes an appendage of the machine, and it is only the most simple, most monotonous, and most easily acquired knack, that is required of him. Hence, the cost of production of a workman is restricted, almost entirely, to the means of subsistence that he requires for his maintenance, and for the propagation of his race. But the price of a commodity, and therefore also of labor, is equal to its cost of production. In proportion, therefore, as the repulsiveness of the work increases, the wage decreases. Nay more, in proportion as the use of machinery and division of labor increases, in the same proportion the burden of toil also increases, whether by prolongation of the working hours, by increase of the work exacted in a given time, or by increased speed of the machinery, etc.

Modern industry has converted the little workshop of the patriarchal master into the great factory of the industrial capitalist. Masses of laborers, crowded into the factory, are organized like soldiers. As privates of the industrial army they are placed under the command of a perfect hierarchy of officers and sergeants. Not only are they slaves of the bourgeois class, and of the bourgeois state; they are daily and hourly enslaved by the machine, by the supervisor, and, above all, by the individual bourgeois manufacturer himself. The more openly this despotism proclaims gain to be its end and aim, the more petty, the more hateful and the more embittering it is. . . .

THE STRUGGLE AND VICTORY OF THE PROLETARIAT

The proletariat goes through various stages of development. With its birth begins its struggle with the bourgeoisie. At first the contest is carried on by individual laborers, then by the work people of a factory, then by the operatives of one trade, in one locality, against the individual bourgeois who directly exploits them. They direct their attacks not against the bourgeois conditions of production, but against the instruments of production themselves; they destroy imported wares that compete with their labor, they smash machinery to pieces, they set factories ablaze, they seek to restore by force the vanished status of the workman of the Middle Ages.

At this stage the laborers still form an incoherent mass scattered over the whole country, and broken up by their mutual competition. If anywhere they unite to form more compact bodies, this is not yet the consequence of their own active union, but of the union of the bourgeoisie, which class, in order to attain its own political ends, is compelled to set the whole proletariat in motion, and is moreover still able to do so for a time. At this stage, therefore, the proletarians do not fight their enemies, but the enemies of their enemies, the remnants of absolute monarchy, the landowners, the nonindustrial bourgeois, the petty bourgeoisie. Thus the whole historical movement is concentrated in the hands of the bourgeoisie; every victory so obtained is a victory for the bourgeoisie.

But with the development of industry the proletariat not only increases in number; it becomes concentrated in greater masses, its strength grows, and it feels that strength more. The various interests and conditions of life within the ranks of the proletariat are more and more equalized, in proportion as machinery obliterates all distinctions of labor and nearly everywhere reduces wages to the same low level. The growing competition among the bourgeois, and the resulting commercial crises, make the wages of the workers ever more fluctuating. The unceasing improvement of machinery, ever more rapidly developing, makes their livelihood more and more precarious; the collisions between individual workmen and individual bourgeois take more and more the character of collisions between two classes. Thereupon the workers begin to form combinations (trade unions) against the bourgeoisie; they club together in order to keep up the rate of wages; they found permanent associations in order to make provision beforehand for these occasional revolts. Here and there the contest breaks out into riots.

Now and then the workers are victorious, but only for a time. The real fruit of their battle lies, not in the immediate results, but in the ever expanding union of the workers. This union is furthered by the improved means of communication which are created by modern industry, and which place the workers of different localities in contact with one another. It was just this contact that was needed to centralize the numerous local struggles, all of the same character, into one national struggle between classes. But every class struggle is a political struggle. And that union, to attain which the burghers of the Middle Ages, with their miserable highways, required centuries, the modern proletarians, thanks to railways, achieve in a few years.

This organization of the proletarians into a class, and consequently into a political party, is continually being upset again by the competition between the workers themselves. But it ever rises up again, stronger, firmer, mightier. It compels legislative recognition of particular interests of the workers, by taking advantage of the divisions among the bourgeoisie itself. Thus the ten-hour bill in England was carried. . . .

Finally, in times when the class struggle nears the decisive hour, the process of dissolution going on within the ruling class, in fact within the whole range of old society, assumes such a violent, glaring character, that a small section of the ruling class cuts itself adrift, and joins the revolutionary class, the class that holds the future in its hands. Just as, therefore, at an earlier period, a section of the nobility went over to the bourgeoisie, so now a portion of the bourgeoisie goes over to the proletariat, and in particular, a portion of the bourgeois ideologists, who have raised themselves to the level of comprehending theoretically the historical movement as a whole.

Of all the classes that stand face to face with the bourgeoisie today, the proletariat alone is a really revolutionary class. The other classes decay and finally disappear in the face of modern industry; the proletariat is its special and essential product. . . .

The social conditions of the old society no longer exist for the proletariat. The proletarian is without property; his relation to his wife and children has no longer anything in common with bourgeois family relations; modern industrial labor, modern subjection to capital, the same in England as in France, in America as in Germany, has stripped him of every trace of national character. Law, morality, religion, are to him so many bourgeois prejudices, behind which lurk in ambush just as many bourgeois interests.

All the preceding classes that got the upper hand, sought to fortify their already acquired status by subjecting society at large to their conditions of appropriation. The proletarians cannot become masters of the productive forces of society, except by abolishing their own previous mode of appropriation, and thereby also every other previous mode of appropriation. They have nothing of their own to secure and to fortify; their mission is to destroy all previous securities for, and insurances of, individual property.

All previous historical movements were movements of minorities, or in the interest of minorities. The proletarian movement is the self-conscious, independent movement of the immense majority, in the interest of the immense majority. The proletariat, the lowest stratum of our present society, cannot stir, cannot raise itself up, without the whole superincumbent strata of official society being sprung into the air. . . .

Hitherto, every form of society has been based, as we have already seen, on the antagonism of oppressing and oppressed classes. But in order to oppress a class, certain conditions must be assured to it under which it can, at least, continue its slavish existence. The serf, in the period of serfdom, raised himself to membership in the commune, just as the petty bourgeois, under the yoke of feudal absolutism, managed to develop into a bourgeois. The modern laborer, on the contrary, instead of rising with the progress of industry, sinks deeper and deeper below the conditions of existence of his own class. He becomes a pauper, and pauperism develops more rapidly than population and wealth. And here it becomes evident, that the bourgeoisie is unfit any longer to be the ruling class in society, and to impose its conditions of existence upon society as an overriding law. It is unfit to rule because it is incompetent to assure an existence to its slave within his slavery, because it cannot help letting him sink into such a state, that it has to feed him, instead of being fed by him. Society can no longer live under this bourgeoisie, in other words, its existence is no longer compatible with society.

The essential condition for the existence and sway of the bourgeois class, is the formation and augmentation of capital; the condition for capital is wage-labor. Wage-labor rests exclusively on competition between the laborers. The advance of industry, whose involuntary promoter is the bourgeoisie, replaces the isolation of the laborers, due to competition, by their revolutionary combination, due to association. The development of modern industry, therefore, cuts from under its feet the very foundation on which the bourgeoisie produces and appropriates products. What the bourgeoisie therefore produces, above all, are its own gravediggers. Its fall and the victory of the proletariat are equally inevitable. . . .

PROPERTY AND FREEDOM

All property relations in the past have continually been subject to historical change consequent upon the change in historical conditions.

The French Revolution, for example, abolished feudal property in favor of bourgeois property.

The distinguishing feature of communism is not the abolition of property generally, but the abolition of bourgeois property. But modern bourgeois private property is the final and most complete expression of the system of producing and appropriating products that is based on class antagonisms, on the exploitation of the many by the few.

In this sense, the theory of the Communists may be summed up in the single sentence: Abolition of private property.

We Communists have been reproached with the desire of abolishing the right of personally acquiring property as the fruit of a man's own labor, which property is alleged to be the groundwork of all personal freedom, activity and independence.

Hard-won, self-acquired, self-earned property! Do you mean the property of the petty artisan and of the small peasant, a form of property that preceded the bourgeois form? There is no need to abolish that; the development of industry has to a great extent already destroyed it, and is still destroying it daily.

Or do you mean modern bourgeois private property?

But does wage-labor create any property for the laborer? Not a bit. It creates capital, *i.e.*, that kind of property which exploits wage-labor, and which cannot increase except upon condition of begetting a new supply of wage-labor for fresh exploitation. Property, in its present form, is based on the antagonism of capital and wage-labor. Let us examine both sides of this antagonism.

To be a capitalist, is to have not only a purely personal, but a social *status* in production. Capital is a collective product, and only by the united action of many members, nay, in the last resort, only by the united action of all members of society, can it be set in motion.

Capital is therefore not a personal, it is a social, power.

When, therefore, capital is converted into common property, into the property of all members of society, personal property is not thereby transformed into social property. It is only the social character of the property that is changed. It loses its class character.

Let us now take wage-labor.

The average price of wage-labor is the minimum wage, *i.e.*, that quantum of the means of subsistence which is absolutely requisite to keep the laborer in bare existence as a laborer. What, therefore, the wage-laborer appropriates by means of his labor, merely suffices to prolong and reproduce a bare existence. We by no means intend to abolish this personal appropriation of the products of labor, an appropriation that is made for the maintenance and reproduction of human life, and that leaves no surplus wherewith to command the labor of others. All that we want to do away with is the miserable character of this appropriation, under which the laborer lives merely to increase capital and is allowed to live only insofar as the interest of the ruling class requires it.

In bourgeois society, living labor is but a means to increase accumulated labor. In Communist society, accumulated labor is but a means to widen, to enrich, to promote the existence of the laborer.

In bourgeois society, therefore, the past dominates the present;

in Communist society, the present dominates the past. In bourgeois society capital is independent and has individuality, while the living person is dependent and has no individuality.

And the abolition of this state of things is called by the bourgeois, abolition of individuality and freedom! And rightly so. The abolition of bourgeois individuality, bourgeois independence, and bourgeois freedom is undoubtedly aimed at.

By freedom is meant, under the present bourgeois conditions of production, free trade, free selling and buying.

But if selling and buying disappears, free selling and buying disappears also. This talk about free selling and buying, and all the other "brave words" of our bourgeoisie about freedom in general, have a meaning, if any, only in contrast with restricted selling and buying, with the fettered traders of the Middle Ages, but have no meaning when opposed to the Communist abolition of buying and selling, of the bourgeois conditions of production, and of the bourgeoisie itself.

You are horrified at our intending to do away with private property. But in your existing society, private property is already done away with for nine-tenths of the population; its existence for the few is solely due to its nonexistence in the hands of those nine-tenths. You reproach us, therefore, with intending to do away with a form of property, the necessary condition for whose existence is the nonexistence of any property for the immense majority of society.

In a word, you reproach us with intending to do away with your property. Precisely so; that is just what we intend.

From the moment when labor can no longer be converted into capital, money, or rent, into a social power capable of being monopolized, *i.e.*, from the moment when individual property can no longer be transformed into bourgeois property, into capital, from that moment, you say, individuality vanishes.

You must, therefore, confess that by "individual" you mean no other person than the bourgeois, than the middle-class owner of property. This person must, indeed, be swept out of the way, and made impossible.

Communism deprives no man of the power to appropriate the products of society; all that it does is to deprive him of the power to subjugate the labor of others by means of such appropriation. . . .

CLASS-RELATIVE CHARACTER OF CULTURE AND IDEOLOGY

All objections urged against the Communist mode of producing and appropriating material products, have, in the same way, been urged against the Communist modes of producing and appropriating intellectual products. Just as, to the bourgeois, the disappearance of class property is the disappearance of production itself, so the disappearance of class culture is to him identical with the disappearance of all culture.

That culture, the loss of which he laments, is, for the enormous majority, a mere training to act as a machine.

But don't wrangle with us so long as you apply, to our intended abolition of bourgeois property, the standard of your bourgeois notions of freedom, culture, law, etc. Your very ideas are but the outgrowth of the conditions of your bourgeois production and bourgeois property, just as your jurisprudence is but the will of your class made into a law for all, a will whose essential character and direction are determined by the economic conditions of existence of your class.

The selfish misconception that induces you to transform into eternal laws of nature and of reason, the social forms springing from your present mode of production and form of property—historical relations that rise and disappear in the progress of production—this misconception you share with every ruling class that has preceded you. What you see clearly in the case of ancient property, what you admit in the case of feudal property, you are of course forbidden to admit in the case of your own bourgeois form of property. . . .

The charges against communism made from a religious, a philosophical, and, generally, from an ideological standpoint, are not deserving of serious examination.

Does it require deep intuition to comprehend that man's ideas, views, and conceptions, in one word, man's consciousness, changes with every change in the conditions of his material existence, in his social relations and in his social life?

What else does the history of ideas prove, than that intellectual production changes its character in proportion as material production is changed? The ruling ideas of each age have ever been the ideas of its ruling class.

When people speak of ideas that revolutionize society, they do but express the fact that within the old society the elements of a new one have been created, and that the dissolution of the old ideas keeps even pace with the dissolution of the old conditions of existence.

When the ancient world was in its last throes, the ancient religions were overcome by Christianity. When Christian ideas succumbed in the eighteenth century to rationalist ideas, feudal society fought its death-battle with the then revolutionary bourgeoisie. The ideas of religious liberty and freedom of conscience, merely gave expression to the sway of free competition within the domain of knowledge.

"Undoubtedly," it will be said, "religion, moral, philosophical and juridical ideas have been modified in the course of historical development. But religion, morality, philosophy, political science, and law, constantly survived this change."

"There are, besides, eternal truths, such as Freedom, Justice, etc., that are common to all states of society. But communism abolishes eternal truths, it abolishes all religion, and all morality, instead of constituting them on a new basis; it therefore acts in contradiction to all past historical experience."

What does this accusation reduce itself to? The history of all past society has consisted in the development of class antagonisms, antagonisms that assumed different forms at different epochs.

But whatever form they may have taken, one fact is common to all past ages, *viz.*, the exploitation of one part of society by the other. No wonder, then, that the social consciousness of past ages, despite all the multiplicity and variety it displays, moves within certain common forms, or general ideas, which cannot completely vanish except with the total disappearance of class antagonisms.

The Communist revolution is the most radical rupture with traditional property relations; no wonder that its development involves the most radical rupture with traditional ideas.

THE PROLETARIAN REVOLUTION

But let us have done with the bourgeois objections to communism.

We have seen above, that the first step in the revolution by the working class, is to raise the proletariat to the position of ruling class, to establish democracy.

The proletariat will use its political supremacy to wrest, by degrees, all capital from the bourgeoisie, to centralize all instruments of production in the hands of the state, *i.e.*, of the proletariat organized as the ruling class; and to increase the total of productive forces as rapidly as possible.

Of course, in the beginning, this cannot be effected except by means of despotic inroads on the rights of property, and on the conditions of bourgeois production; by means of measures, therefore, which appear economically insufficient and untenable, but which, in the course of the movement, outstrip themselves, necessitate further inroads upon the old social order, and are unavoidable as a means of entirely revolutionizing the mode of production. . . .

When, in the course of development, class distinctions have disappeared, and all production has been concentrated in the hands of a vast association of the whole nation, the public power will lose its political character. Political power, properly so called, is merely the organized power of one class for oppressing another. If the proletariat during its contest with the bourgeoisie is compelled, by the force of circumstances, to organize itself as a class; if, by means of a revolution, it makes itself the ruling class, and, as such sweeps away by force the old conditions of production, then it will, along with these conditions, have swept away the conditions for the existence of class antagonisms, and of classes generally, and will thereby have abolished its own supremacy as a class.

In place of the old bourgeois society, with its classes and class antagonisms, we shall have an association, in which the free development of each is the condition for the free development of all.

JOHN STUART MILL

Utilitarian Defense of Individual Liberty

John Stuart Mill, one of the leading English utilitarians, was born in London in 1806. He was given an extraordinary education by his father, *James Mill, a dedicated follower of Jeremy Bentham; the son's precocious accomplishments and accompanying psychological difficulties are described in his* Autobiography. *He became his father's assistant in the East India Company in 1823 and spent the next thirty-five years in that company's employ; during these years he was active also as a writer for several journals. After an association of many years with Mrs. Harriet Taylor, he married her in 1851, seven years before her death. In 1865 Mill was elected to Parliament but was defeated in the election of 1868. He died in Avignon, France in 1873. Nearly all Mill's writings are highly relevant to political philosophy. They include* Utilitarianism, Representative Government, Thoughts on Parliamentary Reform, Chapters on Socialism, Principles of Political Economy (*especially Book V, "On the Influence of Government"*), System of Logic (*especially Book VI, "On the Logic of the Moral Sciences"*), *and* The Subjection of Women. On Liberty *was published in 1859.*

[DEVELOPMENT OF THE IDEA OF POLITICAL LIBERTY][1]

The subject of this Essay is not the so-called Liberty of the Will so unfortunately opposed to the misnamed doctrine of Philosophical Necessity; but Civil, or Social Liberty: the nature and limits of the power which can be legitimately exercised by society over the individual. A question seldom stated, and hardly ever discussed, in general terms, but which profoundly influences the practical controversies of the age by its latent presence, and is likely soon to make itself recognised as the vital question of the future. It is so far from being new, that, in a certain sense, it has divided mankind, almost from the remotest ages; but in the stage of progress into which the more civilised portions of the species have now entered, it presents itself under new conditions, and requires a different and more fundamental treatment.

Selections from *On Liberty.*

[1] From Chapter I.

The struggle between Liberty and Authority is the most conspicuous feature in the portions of history with which we are earliest familiar, particularly in that of Greece, Rome, and England. But in old times this contest was between subjects, or some classes of subjects, and the Government. By liberty, was meant protection against the tyranny of the political rulers. The rulers were conceived (except in some of the popular governments of Greece) as in a necessarily antagonistic position to the people whom they ruled. They consisted of a governing One, or a governing tribe or caste, who derived their authority from the inheritance or conquest, who, at all events, did not hold it at the pleasure of the governed, and whose supremacy men did not venture, perhaps did not desire, to contest, whatever precautions might be taken against its oppressive exercise. Their power was regarded as necessary, but also as highly dangerous; as a weapon which they would attempt to use against their subjects, no less than against external enemies. To prevent the weaker members of the community from being preyed upon by innumerable vultures, it was needful that there should be an animal of prey stronger than the rest, commissioned to keep them down. But as the king of the vultures would be no less bent upon preying on the flock than any of the minor harpies, it was indispensable to be in a perpetual attitude of defence against his beak and claws. The aim, therefore, of patriots was to set limits to the power which the ruler should be suffered to exercise over the community; and this limitation was what they meant by liberty. It was attempted in two ways. First, by obtaining a recognition of certain immunities, called political liberties or rights, which it was to be regarded as a breach of duty in the ruler to infringe, and which if he did infringe, specific resistance, or general rebellion, was held to be justifiable. A second, and generally a later expedient, was the establishment of constitutional checks, by which the consent of the community, or of a body of some sort, supposed to represent its interests, was made a necessary condition to some of the more important acts of the governing power. To the first of these modes of limitation, the ruling power, in most European countries, was compelled, more or less, to submit. It was not so with the second; and, to attain this, or when already in some degree possessed, to attain it more completely, became everywhere the principal object of the lovers of liberty. And so long as mankind were content to combat one enemy by another, and to be ruled by a master, on condition of being guaranteed more or less efficaciously against his tyranny, they did not carry their aspirations beyond this point.

A time, however, came, in the progress of human affairs, when men ceased to think it a necessity of nature that their governors should be an independent power, opposed in interest to themselves. It appeared to them much better that the various magistrates of the State should be their tenants or delegates, revocable at their pleasure. In that way alone, it seemed, could they have complete security that the powers of government would never be abused to their disadvantage. By degrees this new demand for elective and temporary rulers became the prominent object of the exertions of the popular party, wherever any such party existed; and superseded, to a considerable extent, the previous efforts to limit the power of rulers. As the struggle proceeded for making the ruling power emanate from the periodical choice of the ruled, some persons began to think that too much importance had been attached to the limitation of the power itself. *That* (it might seem) was a resource against rulers whose interests were habitually opposed to those of the people. What was now wanted was, that the rulers should be identified with the people; that their interest and will should be the interest and will of the nation. The nation did not need to be protected against its own will. There was no fear of its tyrannising over itself. Let the rulers be effectually responsible to it, promptly removable by it, and it could afford to trust them with power of which it could itself dictate the use to be made. Their power was but the nation's own power, concentrated, and in a form convenient for exercise. This mode of thought, or rather perhaps of feeling, was common among the last generation of European liberalism, in the Continental section of which it still apparently predominates. Those who admit any limit to what a government may do, except in the case of such governments as they think ought not to exist, stand out as brilliant exceptions among the political thinkers of the Continent. A similar tone of sentiment might by this time have been prevalent in our own country, if the circumstances which for a time encouraged it, had continued unaltered.

[THE TYRANNY OF THE MAJORITY]

But, in political and philosophical theories, as well as in persons, success discloses faults and infirmities which failure might have concealed from observation. The notion, that the people have no need to limit their power over themselves, might seem axiomatic, when popular government was a thing only dreamed about, or read of as having existed at some distant period of the past. Neither was the notion necessarily disturbed by such temporary aberrations as those of the French Revolution, the worst of which were the work of a usurping few, and which, in any case, belonged, not to the permanent working of popular institutions, but to a sudden and convulsive outbreak against monarchical and aristocratic despotism. In time, however, a democratic republic came to occupy a large portion of the earth's surface, and made itself felt as one of the most powerful members of the community of nations; and elective and responsible government became subject to the observations and criticisms which wait upon a great existing fact. It was now perceived that such phrases as "self-government," and "the power of the people over themselves," do not express the true state of the case. The "people" who exercise the power are not always the same people with those over whom it is exercised; and the "self-government" spoken of is not the government of each by himself, but of each by all the rest. The will of the people, moreover, practically means the will of the most numerous or the most active *part* of the people; the majority, or those who succeed in making themselves accepted as the majority; the people, consequently *may* desire to oppress a part of their number; and precautions are as much needed against this as against any other abuse of power. The limitation, therefore, of the power of government over individuals loses none of its importance when the holders of power are regularly accountable to the community, that is, to the strongest party therein. This view of things, recommending itself equally to the intelligence of thinkers and to the inclination of those important classes in European society to whose real or supposed interests democracy is adverse, has had no difficulty in establishing itself; and in political speculations "the tyranny of the majority" is now generally included among the evils against which society requires to be on its guard.

Like other tyrannies the tyranny of the majority was at first, and is still vulgarly, held in dread, chiefly as operating through the acts of the public authorities But reflecting persons perceived that when society is itself the tyrant—society collectively over the separate individuals who compose it—its means of tyrannising are not restricted to the acts which it may do by the hands of its political functionaries. Society can and does execute its own mandates: and if it issues wrong mandates instead of right, or any mandates at all in things with which it ought not to meddle, it practises a social tyranny more formidable than many kinds of political oppression, since, though not usually upheld by such extreme penalties, it leaves fewer means of escape, penetrating much more deeply into the details of life, and enslaving the soul itself. Protection, therefore, against the tyranny of the magistrate is not enough: there needs protection also against the tyranny of the prevailing opinion and feeling; against the tendency of society to impose, by other means than civil penalties, its own ideas and practices as rules of conduct on those who dissent from them; to fetter the development, and, if possible, prevent the formation, of any individuality not in harmony with its ways, and compel all characters to fashion themselves upon the model of its own. There is a limit to the legitimate interference of collective opinion with individual independence: and to find that limit, and maintain it against encroachment, is as indispensable to a good condition of human affairs, as protection against political despotism. . . .

[THE PRINCIPLE OF INDIVIDUAL LIBERTY]

The object of this Essay is to assert one very simple principle, as entitled to govern absolutely the dealings of society with the individual in the way of compulsion and control, whether the means used be physical force in the form of legal penalties, or the moral coercion of public opinion. That principle is, that the sole end for which mankind are warranted, individually or collectively, in interfering with the liberty of action of any of their number, is self-protection. That the only purpose for which power can be rightfully exercised over any member of a civilised community, against his will, is to prevent harm to others. His own good, either physical or moral, is not a sufficient warrant. He cannot rightfully be compelled to do or forbear because it will be better for him to do so, because it will make him happier, because, in the opinions of others, to do so would be wise, or even right. These are good reasons for remonstrating with him, or reasoning with him, or persuading him, or entreating him, but not for compelling him, or visiting him with any evil in case he do otherwise. To justify that, the conduct from which it is desired to deter him must be calculated to produce evil to some one else. The only part of the conduct of any one, for which he is amenable to society, is that which concerns others. In the part which merely concerns himself, his independence is, of right, absolute. Over himself, over his own body and mind, the individual is sovereign.

It is, perhaps hardly necessary to say that this doctrine is meant to apply only to human beings in the maturity of their faculties. We are not speaking of children, or of young persons below the age which the law may fix as that of manhood or womanhood. Those who are still in a state to require being taken care of by others, must be protected against their own actions as well as against external injury. For the same reason, we may leave out of consideration those backward states of society in which the race itself may be considered as in its nonage. The early difficulties in the way of spontaneous progress are so great, that there is seldom any choice of means for overcoming them; and a ruler full of the spirit of improvement is warranted in the use of any expedients that will attain an end, perhaps otherwise unattainable. Despotism is a legitimate mode of government in dealing with barbarians, provided the end be their improvement, and the means justified by actually effecting that end. Liberty, as a principle, has no application to any state of things anterior to the time when mankind have become capable of being improved by free and equal discussion. Until then, there is nothing for them but implicit obedience to an Akbar or a Charlemagne, if they are so fortunate as to find one. But as soon as mankind have attained the capacity of being guided to their own improvement by conviction or persuasion (a period long since reached in all nations with whom we need here concern ourselves), compulsion, either in the direct form or in that of pains and penalties for non-compliance, is no longer admissible as a means to their own good, and justifiable only for the security of others.

It is proper to state that I forego any advantage which could be derived to my argument from the idea of abstract right, as a thing independent of utility. I regard utility as the ultimate appeal on all ethical questions; but it must be utility in the largest sense, grounded on the permanent interests of a man as a progressive being. Those interests, I contend, authorise the subjection of individual spontaneity to external control, only in respect to those actions of each, which concern the interest of other people. If any one does an act hurtful to others, there is a *prima facie* case for punishing him, by law, or, where legal penalties are not safely applicable, by general disapprobation. There are also many positive acts for the benefit of others, which he may rightfully be compelled to perform; such as to give evidence in a court of justice; to bear his fair share in the common defence, or in any other joint work necessary to the interest of the society of which he enjoys the protection; and to perform certain acts of individual beneficence, such as saving a fellow-creature's life, or interposing to protect the defenceless against ill-usage, things which whenever it is obviously a man's duty to do, he may rightfully be made responsible to society for not doing. A person may cause evil to others not only by his actions but by his inaction, and in either case he is justly accountable to them for the injury. The latter case, it is true, requires a much more cautious exercise of compulsion than the former. To make any one answerable for doing evil to others is the rule; to make him answerable for not preventing evil is, comparatively speaking, the exception. Yet there are many cases clear enough and grave enough to justify that exception. In all things which regard the external relations of the individual, he is *de jure* amenable to those whose interests are concerned, and, if need be, to society as their protector. There are often good reasons for not holding him to the responsibility; but these reasons must arise from the special expediencies of the case: either because it is a kind of case in which he is on the whole likely to act better, when left to his own discretion, than when controlled in any way in which society have it in their power to control him; or because the attempt to exercise control would produce other evils, greater than those which it would prevent. When such reasons as these preclude the enforcement of responsibility, the conscience of the agent himself should step into the vacant judgment seat, and protect those interests of others which have no external protection; judging himself all the more rigidly, because the case does not admit of his being made accountable to the judgment of his fellow-creatures.

But there is a sphere of action in which society, as distinguished from the individual, has, if any, only an indirect interest; comprehending all that portion of a person's life and conduct which affects only himself, or if it also affects others, only with their free, voluntary, and undeceived consent and participation. When I say only himself, I mean directly, and in the first instance; for whatever affects himself, may affect others through himself; and the objection

which may be grounded on this contingency, will receive consideration in the sequel. This, then, is the appropriate region of human
liberty. It comprises, first, the inward domain of consciousness;
demanding liberty of conscience in the most comprehensive sense;
liberty of thought and feeling; absolute freedom of opinion and
sentiment on all subjects, practical or speculative, scientific, moral,
or theological. The liberty of expressing and publishing opinions
may seem to fall under a different principle, since it belongs to that
part of the conduct of an individual which concerns other people;
but, being almost of as much importance as the liberty of thought
itself, and resting in great part on the same reasons, is practically
inseparable from it. Secondly, the principle requires liberty of tastes
and pursuits; of framing the plan of our life to suit our own character; of doing as we like, subject to such consequences as may follow;
without impediment from our fellow-creatures, so long as what we
do does not harm them, even though they should think our conduct
foolish, perverse, or wrong. Thirdly, from this liberty of each individual, follows the liberty, within the same limits, of combination
among individuals; freedom to unite, for any purpose not involving
harm to others; the persons combining being supposed to be of full
age, and not forced or deceived.

No society in which these liberties are not, on the whole, re-
spected, is free, whatever may be its form of government; and none
is completely free in which they do not exist absolute and unqualified. The only freedom which deserves the name, is that of pursuing our own good in our own way, so long as we do not attempt
to deprive others of theirs, or impede their efforts to obtain it. Each
is the proper guardian of his own health, whether bodily, or mental
and spiritual. Mankind are greater gainers by suffering each other
to live as seems good to themselves, than by compelling each to
live as seems good to the rest. . . .

LIBERTY OF THOUGHT AND
DISCUSSION [2]

We have now recognised the necessity to the mental well-being
of mankind (on which all their other well-being depends) of
freedom of opinion, and freedom of the expression of opinion, on
four distinct grounds; which we will now briefly recapitulate.

First, if any opinion is compelled to silence, that opinion may,

[2] From Chapter II.

for aught we can certainly know, be true. To deny this is to assume our own infallibility.

Secondly, though the silenced opinion be an error, it may, and very commonly does, contain a portion of truth; and since the general or prevailing opinion on any subject is rarely or never the whole truth, it is only by the collision of adverse opinions that the remainder of the truth has any chance of being supplied.

Thirdly, even if the received opinion be not only true, but the whole truth; unless it is suffered to be, and actually is, vigorously and earnestly contested, it will, by most of those who receive it, be held in the manner of a prejudice, with little comprehension or feeling of its rational grounds. And not only this, but, fourthly, the meaning of the doctrine itself will be in danger of being lost, or enfeebled, and deprived of its vital effect on the character and conduct; the dogma becoming a mere formal profession, inefficacious for good, but cumbering the ground, and preventing the growth of any real and heartfelt conviction, from reason or personal experience.

Before quitting the subject of freedom of opinion, it is fit to take some notice of those who say that the free expression of all opinions should be permitted, on condition that the manner be temperate, and do not pass the bounds of fair discussion. Much might be said on the impossibility of fixing where these supposed bounds are to be placed; for if the test be offence to those whose opinions are attacked, I think experience testifies that this offence is given whenever the attack is telling and powerful, and that every opponent who pushes them hard, and whom they find it difficult to answer, appears to them, if he shows any strong feeling on the subject, an intemperate opponent. . . . The worst offence of this kind which can be committed by a polemic is to stigmatise those who hold the contrary opinion as bad and immoral men. To calumny of this sort, those who hold any unpopular opinion are peculiarly exposed, because they are in general few and uninfluential, and nobody but themselves feels much interested in seeing justice done them; but this weapon is, from the nature of the case, denied to those who attack a prevailing opinion: they can neither use it with safety to themselves, nor, if they could, would it do anything but recoil on their own cause. In general, opinions contrary to those commonly received can only obtain a hearing by studied moderation of language, and the most cautious avoidance of unnecessary offence, from which they hardly ever deviate even in a slight degree without losing ground: while unmeasured vituperation employed on the side of the prevailing opinion really does deter people from professing contrary opinions, and from listening to those who profess them. For the interest, therefore, of truth and justice, it is far more important to restrain this employment of vituperative language than the other; and, for example, if it were necessary to choose, there would be much more need to discourage offensive attacks on infidelity than on religion. It is, however, obvious that law and authority have no business with restraining either . . .

OF INDIVIDUALITY, AS ONE OF THE ELEMENTS OF WELL-BEING [3]

Such being the reasons which make it imperative that human beings should be free to form opinions, and to express their opinions without reserve; and such the baneful consequences to the intellectual, and through that to the moral nature of man, unless this liberty is either conceded, or asserted in spite of prohibition; let us next examine whether the same reasons do not require that men should be free to act upon their opinions—to carry these out in their lives, without hindrance, either physical or moral, from their fellow-men, so long as it is at their own risk and peril. This last proviso is of course indispensable. No one pretends that actions should be as free as opinions. On the contrary, even opinions lose their immunity when the circumstances in which they are expressed are such as to constitute their expression a positive instigation to some mischievous act. An opinion that corn-dealers are starvers of the poor, or that private property is robbery, ought to be unmolested when simply circulated through the press, but may justly incur punishment when delivered orally to an excited mob assembled before the house of a corn-dealer, or when handed about among the same mob in the form of a placard. Acts, of whatever kind, which, without justifiable cause, do harm to others, may be, and in the more important cases absolutely require to be, controlled by the unfavourable sentiments, and, when needful, by the active interference of mankind. The liberty of the individual must be thus far limited; he must not make himself a nuisance to other people. But if he refrains from molesting others in what concerns them, and merely acts according to his own inclination and judgment in things which concern himself, the same reasons which show

[3] From Chapter III.

that opinion should be free, prove also that he should be allowed, without molestation, to carry his opinions into practice at his own cost. . . . As it is useful that while mankind are imperfect there should be different opinions, so it is that there should be different experiments of living; that free scope should be given to varieties of character, short of injury to others; and that the worth of different modes of life should be proved practically, when any one thinks fit to try them. It is desirable, in short, that in things which do not primarily concern others, individuality should assert itself. Where, not the person's own character, but the traditions or customs of other people are the rule of conduct, there is wanting one of the principal ingredients of human happiness, and quite the chief ingredient of individual and social progress.

In maintaining this principle, the greatest difficulty to be encountered does not lie in the appreciation of means towards an acknowledged end, but in the indifference of persons in general to the end itself. If it were felt that the free development of individuality is one of the leading essentials of well-being; that it is not only a co-ordinate element with all that is designated by the terms civilisation, instruction, education, culture, but is itself a necessary part and condition of all those things; there would be no danger that liberty should be undervalued, and the adjustment of the boundaries between it and social control would present no extraordinary difficulty. But the evil is, that individual spontaneity is hardly recognised by the common modes of thinking as having any intrinsic worth, or deserving any regard on its own account. The majority, being satisfied with the ways of mankind as they now are (for it is they who make them what they are), cannot comprehend why those ways should not be good enough for everybody; and what is more, spontaneity forms no part of the ideal of the majority of moral and social reformers, but is rather looked on with jealousy, as a troublesome and perhaps rebellious obstruction to the general acceptance of what these reformers, in their own judgment, think would be best for mankind. Few persons, out of Germany, even comprehend the meaning of the doctrine which Wilhelm von Humboldt, so eminent both as a *savant* and as a politician, made the text of a treatise—that "the end of man, or that which is prescribed by the eternal or immutable dictates of reason, and not suggested by vague and transient desires, is the highest and most harmonious development of his powers to a complete and consistent whole;" that, therefore, the object "towards which every human being must ceaselessly direct his efforts, and on which especially those who design to influence their fellow-men must ever keep their eyes, is the individuality of power and development;" that for this there are two requisites, "freedom, and variety of situations;" and that from the union of these arise "individual vigour and manifold diversity," which combine themselves in "originality."

[SELF-REGARDING AND OTHER-REGARDING ACTIONS] [4]

The distinction here pointed out between the part of a person's life which concerns only himself, and that which concerns others, many persons will refuse to admit. How (it may be asked) can any part of the conduct of a member of society be a matter of indifference to the other members? No person is an entirely isolated being; it is impossible for a person to do anything seriously or permanently hurtful to himself, without mischief reaching at least to his near connections, and often far beyond them. If he injures his property, he does harm to those who directly or indirectly derived support from it, and usually diminishes, by a greater or less amount, the general resources of the community. If he deteriorates his bodily or mental faculties, he not only brings evil upon all who depended on him for any portion of their happiness, but disqualifies himself for rendering the services which he owes to his fellow-creatures generally; perhaps becomes a burthen on their affection or benevolence; and if such conduct were very frequent, hardly any offence that is committed would detract more from the general sum of good. Finally, if by his vices or follies a person does no direct harm to others, he is nevertheless (it may be said) injurious by his example; and ought to be compelled to control himself, for the sake of those whom the sight or knowledge of his conduct might corrupt or mislead.

And even (it will be added) if the consequences of misconduct could be confined to the vicious or thoughtless individual, ought society to abandon to their own guidance those who are manifestly unfit for it? If protection against themselves is confessedly due to children and persons under age, is not society equally bound to afford it to persons of mature years who are equally incapable of

[4] From Chapter IV.

self-government? If gambling, or drunkenness, or incontinence, or idleness, or uncleanliness, are as injurious to happiness, and as great a hindrance to improvement, as many or most of the acts prohibited by law, why (it may be asked) should not law, so far as is consistent with practicability and social convenience, endeavour to repress these also? . . .

I fully admit that the mischief which a person does to himself may seriously affect, both through their sympathies and their interests, those nearly connected with him and, in a minor degree, society at large. When, by conduct of this sort, a person is led to violate a distinct and assignable obligation to any other person or persons, the case is taken out of the self-regarding class, and becomes amenable to moral disapprobation in the proper sense of the term. If, for example, a man, through intemperance or extravagance, becomes unable to pay his debts, or, having undertaken the moral responsibility of a family, becomes from the same cause incapable of supporting or educating them, he is deservedly reprobated, and might be justly punished; but it is for the breach of duty to his family or creditors, not for the extravagance. . . . In like manner, when a person disables himself, by conduct purely self-regarding, from the performance of some definite duty incumbent on him to the public, he is guilty of a social offence. No person ought to be punished simply for being drunk; but a soldier or a policeman should be punished for being drunk on duty. Whenever, in short, there is a definite damage, or a definite risk of damage, either to an individual or to the public, the case is taken out of the province of liberty, and placed in that of morality or law.

But with regard to the merely contingent, or, as it may be called, constructive injury which a person causes to society, by conduct which neither violates any specific duty to the public, nor occasions perceptible hurt to any assignable individual except himself; the inconvenience is one which society can afford to bear, for the sake of the greater good of human freedom. . . .

[NO FREEDOM TO ALIENATE FREEDOM] [5]

It was pointed out in an early part of this Essay, that the liberty of the individual, in things wherein the individual is alone concerned, implies a corresponding liberty in any number of individuals to regulate by mutual agreement such things as regard them jointly,

[5] From Chapter V.

and regard no persons but themselves. This question presents no difficulty, so long as the will of all the persons implicated remains unaltered; but since that will may change, it is often necessary, even in things in which they alone are concerned, that they should enter into engagements with one another; and when they do, it is fit, as a general rule, that those engagements should be kept. Yet, in the laws, probably, of every country, this general rule has some exceptions. Not only persons are not held to engagements which violate the rights of third parties, but it is sometimes considered a sufficient reason for releasing them from an engagement, that it is injurious to themselves. In this and most other civilised countries, for example, an engagement by which a person should sell himself, or allow himself to be sold, as a slave, would be null and void; neither enforced by law nor by opinion. The ground for thus limiting his power of voluntarily disposing of his own lot in life, is apparent, and is very clearly seen in this extreme case. The reason for not interfering, unless for the sake of others, with a person's voluntary acts, is consideration for his liberty. His voluntary choice is evidence that what he so chooses is desirable, or at least endurable, to him, and his good is on the whole best provided for by allowing him to take his own means of pursuing it. But by selling himself for a slave, he abdicates his liberty; he foregoes any future use of it beyond that single act. He therefore defeats, in his own case, the very purpose which is the justification of allowing him to dispose of himself. He is no longer free; but is thenceforth in a position which has no longer the presumption in its favour, that would be afforded by his voluntarily remaining in it. The principle of freedom cannot require that he should be free not to be free. It is not freedom to be allowed to alienate his freedom.

Bibliography

The student would be well advised to read at least some of the complete works from which selections have been excerpted. All of them, except Hegel's *Philosophy of Right,* are available in low-priced paperback or cloth-covered editions, or both. Other major classics of political philosophy which have frequently been referred to in the Introduction are Plato's *Republic,* Aristotle's *Politics,* Thomas Aquinas' "Treatise on Law" (*Summa Theologica,* II, I, questions 90–97), David Hume's *Treatise of Human Nature* (Book III, Parts I and II) and his *Political Essays* (especially "Of the Original Contract"), Immanuel Kant's *Philosophy of Law,* and Jeremy Bentham's *Principles of Morals and Legislation.* All of these works are available in low-priced editions.

POSITIVISTIC APPROACHES TO POLITICAL PHILOSOPHY

While the emphasis in this volume has been on political philosophy as a branch of moral philosophy, there also exists a "positivistic" tradition which approaches basic problems of politics from a nonmoral and often an amoral point of view (see the Introduction, Section V, first paragraph). This approach is exhibited in part in the selections from Hobbes and Marx-Engels, but its most famous representative is Machiavelli's *The Prince* (available in several editions; see especially Chaps. XV–XVIII). The ancestry of this approach in Western thought goes back to the. Greek sophists (see, for example, the first two books of Plato's *Republic*), but it is also found in various parts of Aristotle's *Politics,* especially in Book V, Chap. xi, where Aristotle discusses how tyrants should proceed in order to preserve their power against revolutionary overthrow. A different kind of positivistic approach is found in some parts of St. Augustine's *City of God* (trans. M. Dods, Modern Library Giant), especially Books IV and XIX.

For recent positivistic approaches, the "elitists" in particular may be consulted. Representatives are R. Michels, *Political Parties: A Sociological Study of the Oligarchical Tendencies of Modern Democracy* (Glencoe, Ill.: Free Press, 1949); G. Mosca, *The Ruling Class* (New York: McGraw-Hill, 1939); and H. D. Lasswell, *Politics: Who Gets What, When, How* (New York: Meridian, 1958). These works merge directly into the "behavioralist" approach which is widely followed among contemporary American political scientists, although there are also some important differences. See further various logical-empirical confrontations of traditional ideals with contemporary realities, such as R. A. Dahl, *A Preface to Democratic Theory* (Chicago: Univ. of Chicago Press, 1956).

UTILITARIAN AND DEONTOLOGICAL CRITERIA OF MORALITY

Good recent texts which should help introduce the student to the current state of interpretation of these criteria are R. B. Brandt, *Ethical Theory* (Englewood Cliffs, N.J.: Prentice-Hall, 1959), Chaps. 14–15; J. Hospers, *Human Conduct* (New York: Harcourt, Brace and World, 1961), Chaps. 5–7; W. K. Frankena, *Ethics* (Englewood Cliffs, N.J.: Prentice-Hall, 1963), Chaps. 2–3.

BASIC QUESTIONS OF POLITICAL PHILOSOPHY

As against the historically oriented discussion of the basic questions in the Introduction, I have elsewhere presented a more analytical discussion of them: A. Gewirth, "Political Justice," in R. B. Brandt (ed.), *Social Justice* (Englewood Cliffs, N.J.: Prentice-Hall, 1962), pp. 119–169. (See also the other four essays in the Brandt-edited volume.) While these basic questions are often not explicitly distinguished, they figure prominently in recent writings in political philosophy, including many discussions of democracy, civil rights and liberties, and the welfare state. See, for example, J. Plamenatz, *Consent, Freedom, and Political Obligation* (Oxford Univ. Press, 1938); I. Berlin, *Two Concepts of Liberty* (Oxford: Clarendon Press, 1958); S. Hook, *The Paradoxes of Freedom* (Berkeley: Univ. of California Press, 1962); F. A. Hayek, *The Constitution of Liberty* (Chicago: Univ. of Chicago Presss, 1960); H. L. A. Hart, *Law, Liberty, and Morality* (Stanford: Stanford Univ. Press, 1963); H. Wechsler, *Principles, Politics, and Fundamental Law* (Cambridge, Mass.: Harvard Univ. Press, 1961).

ALTERNATIVE INTERPRETATIONS OF CLASSICAL POLITICAL PHILOSOPHERS

The student's understanding of the great political philosophers will be sharpened if he is aware of some of the conflicting ways in which they have been interpreted and evaluated. For Hobbes see H. Warrender, *The Political Philosophy of Hobbes: His Theory of Obligation* (Oxford: Clarendon, 1957). For Locke see W. Kendall, *John Locke and the Doctrine of Majority Rule* (Urbana: Univ. of Illinois Press, 1941) and J. W. Gough, *John Locke's Political Philosophy* (Oxford: Clarendon, 1950). For Rousseau see J. Talmon, *The Rise of Totalitarian Democracy* (Boston: Beacon, 1952) and J. W. Chapman, *Rousseau: Totalitarian or Liberal?* (New York: Columbia Univ. Press, 1956). For Hegel see H. Marcuse, *Reason and Revolution: Hegel and the Rise of Social Theory* (Boston: Beacon, 1960), especially pp. 178–223, 409–419; and K. R.

Popper, *The Open Society and Its Enemies* (New York: Harper [Harper Torchbooks], 1962), Vol. II, Chap. xii (Popper's work on Hegel must be used with great caution). For Marx see S. Hook, *The Ambiguous Legacy: Marx and the Marxists* (New York: Van Nostrand, 1955); S. W. Moore, *The Critique of Capitalist Democracy* (New York: Paine-Whitman, 1957); R. Tucker, *Philosophy and Myth in Karl Marx* (London: Cambridge Univ. Press, 1961). For Mill, see J. C. Rees, *Mill and His Early Critics* (Leicester: University College, 1956).

THE LOGIC OF POLITICAL LANGUAGE AND OF POLITICAL PHILOSOPHY

As against the extensive work by analytic philosophers on the logic of moral language, comparatively little has been written on the corresponding problems of political language and argument. See T. D. Weldon, *The Vocabulary of Politics* (Baltimore: Penguin, 1953), a highly provocative, but for the most part unsatisfactory, polemic; M. Macdonald, "The Language of Political Theory," and H. L. A. Hart, "The Ascription of Rights and Responsibilities," both in A. Flew (ed.), *Logic and Language* (First Series; Oxford: Blackwell, 1951), pp. 145–186; S. I. Benn and R. S. Peters, *Social Principles and the Democratic State* (London: Allen & Unwin, 1959); the two series edited by P. Laslett, *Philosophy, Politics and Society* (Oxford: Blackwell, 1956, 1962); and various essays in the yearbook volumes of the American Society for Political and Legal Philosophy, *Nomos,* ed. C. J. Friedrich, (seven volumes published so far). A comprehensive survey from the standpoint of "scientific value-relativism" is A. Brecht, *Political Theory: The Foundations of Twentieth-Century Political Thought* (Princeton, N.J.: Princeton Univ. Press, 1959). See also such analyses of specific concepts as A. I. Melden, *Rights and Right Conduct* (Oxford: Blackwell, 1959) and F. E. Oppenheim, *Dimensions of Freedom: An Analysis* (New York: St Martin's, 1961). For an empirical approach, see H. D. Lasswell et al., *Language of Politics: Studies in Quantitative Semantics* (New York: G. W. Stewart, 1949). Still useful are such classics as J. Bentham, *Handbook of Political Fallacies* (New York: Harper Torchbooks, 1962) and G. Cornewall Lewis, *Remarks on the Use and Abuse of Political Terms* (Oxford: Clarendon, 1898).